Taareef us khuda ki jisne jahan banaya
Kaisee zameen banayi kya aasman banaya

Sooraj se humnein payee hai garmee bhi roshni bhi
Kya khoob chashma toone ay meherbaan banaya

Pairon taley bichhaya kya khoob farsh khaki
Aur sar pe laaj wardi ek saaibaan banaya

Rehmat se tere kya kya hai neemat-e-mayyassar
In neematon ka mujhko kya qadrdaan banaya

Mittee say bael bootay kya khushnumaan ugaye
Pehna ke sabz khilat unko jawan banaya

SARDAR AMAR SINGH WHO RECOGNIZED
HIS SON'S LOVE FOR MUSIC

1

The year was 1941. There was nothing to indicate what the future held. Nothing unusual. Amar Singh's wife, Bachan Kaur, had borne him the third of their eleven children.

Perhaps, when this baby cried, his voice held a different quality, but in a house full of children, and with so many chores waiting to be attended to, who had the time to notice?

In due course, the ceremonies that marked the first milestones of a child's life were duly held. The newborn was given a name, Jagmohan—one who charms the world. And life went on, a river meandering through the peaks and valleys of daily living. Later, the young Jagmohan's name would be changed to Jagjit Singh.

Jagjit's father, Amar Singh, was born a Hindu. But the young Amin Chand, as he had been named by his parents, found himself drawn to the teachings of the Sikh Gurus. What his parents felt about his conversion to Sikhism—growing his hair and adopting a turban and the other signs of his new religion—is unknown, but the seventeen-year-old took the tenets of Sikhism seriously. Changing his name to Amar Singh, he joined the Namdhari sect. The Namdhari Sikhs believe in the purity of word, thought and deed. They are passionate about the protection of animals and practise vegetarianism. Amar Singh held all these tenets close to his heart; he turned vegetarian and lived his life with honest piety.

Working hard to rise from the poverty he had been born into, Amar Singh worked by day and studied by night, and finally found himself a job in the Public Works Department. It was a job that spelt security and a certain degree of comfort. He was sent to Bikaner, where he would set up home.

His wife, addressed as Beeji by everyone, came from a family better off than his. A chance encounter resulted in their marriage. A meeting on a train between two passengers, an exchange of family stories, and

A young Jagmohan Singh riding pillion

JAGJIT SINGH WITH HIS YOUNGER SISTERS

Amar Singh was betrothed. He soon found himself in the new role of husband and householder.

Following the rules laid down by his Gurus, Amar Singh presided over a household that was spartan in its lifestyle to the extent that tea and other mood-enhancing drinks were forbidden to its members. Yet, he was a man known for his generosity. He believed in sharing whatever little he had with friends and relatives who passed in and out of his home, and with his many children. He would father eleven in the course of his married life, and be a strict and firm father to the seven who survived.

The Singh family lived a quiet but industrious life. Amar Singh provided for his family while his wife cooked, sewed clothes and busied herself with the endless cycles of housekeeping chores and tasks that concerned her children. If they noticed that the tenor of their lives improved after the birth of Jagmohan, no one made much of it. Though Amar Singh would mention the fact much later, prompted perhaps by what the future brought to his experience.

Perhaps the first intimation that, of all his children, Jagmohan would be the most distinctive one, came to Amar Singh when the family's Namdhari Guru advised him to change Jagmohan's name to Jagjit. 'He will win the world over,' the Guru predicted. Obediently, the boy's name was changed. Jagjit Singh was formally born.

Whether the world would be conquered by Jagjit's sword or pen, or whether he had the makings of an administrator, was not a matter of conjecture. Jagjit did what his brothers did: he went to school where he learnt to read and write in Urdu, and was taught how to do his sums. The school was humble and the children sat cross-legged on the floor and wrote on slates. In the evenings, studies would continue by the dim light of lanterns.

Music was not a part of their daily life, at least not in the way it is today. 'Radios were a luxury not everyone could afford,' Jagjit Singh had said of his early years. 'World War II was on, and I remember going for walks with my father to the park so that we could overhear the news on the radio from a nearby house.'*

His first encounter with music must have been at the singing of the Gurbani. The ragas that accompanied the sacred words of the Gurus would have become familiar by repetition. Amar Singh loved the sound of music, and

**Jagjit Singh's quotes have been taken from the book* Beyond Time, *a limited edition published by Pankaj Kodesia & Associates in 2002*

decided that at least some of his children should learn it formally, for their own understanding of its intricacies and for the joys music could bring.

He chose Jagjit. The boy seemed to have a natural love for music. When the family moved to Sri Ganganagar, where Amar Singh originally hailed from, circumstances seemed to have changed for the better. Among the trappings of an easier life was the presence of a radio, as much to keep abreast of the news as to provide relief from the monotony of daily chores.

Jagjit, especially, was entranced by the songs that played on the radio from the films of the time. The twelve-year-old would listen intently and sing as he went about his share of household jobs, which included carrying water from the well, buying vegetables, or running errands.

His singing did not go unnoticed. It led to his first formal lesson. To his delight, he was taken to the blind singer, Pandit Chhaganlal Sharma, to learn classical music. Jagjit proved a good pupil, listening with a keen ear, dedicating himself to absorbing all that his teacher taught him. Soon enough, there was little else he could learn from the Pandit. Once he had mastered the basics, Jagjit was taken to Ustad Jamal Khan, who would take the lessons forward, teaching him thumri and khayal. He could not have asked for a teacher with a more impressive lineage, for the Ustad claimed descent from the legendary Tansen himself.

Jagjit's youngest brother, Kartar Singh, who lives in Delhi and runs the very successful Hao Shi Nian Nian restaurant that specializes in Chinese cuisine, remembers how his brother would sit for hours on end with the Ustad, learning greedily whatever the teacher could offer. 'He was full of *shararat*, some of it unprintable here,' Kartar recollects, 'but when it came to music, he turned into another person. We would be playing, but when Khan sahib came, he would rush to him, hair still open, in his dirty, sweaty clothes, and sit down for the lesson. Ustad-ji carried a thin, long stick, and if Jagjit made a mistake, he would rap him with it on the knuckles. We would be drawn by the lesson, and sit around them. Very quietly. Otherwise, we would be banished.'

Kartar clearly remembers the sight of his brother sitting long after the Ustad had left, practising for hours, tanpura strumming along to keep his voice company. 'At home, all of us liked listening to him practise, but none of us sang. I understood nothing of the music but appreciated it nonetheless, and though I was told I had a good voice, I could not bend myself to the demands of riyaz. My eldest brother played the tabla, though.'

Jagjit learnt from the venerable Ustad Jamal Khan of the Senia gharana what he treasured as his favourite bandishes. The Ustad also taught him dhrupads in Malkauns and Bilaskhani Todi. Jagjit did not realize the value of these lessons until later, when they helped him along in his musical journey.

Though closest to Jagjit among his siblings, Kartar lost daily contact with Jagjit while he was still in class three, when the elder brother moved to Jalandhar for higher studies. 'But the bond remained, and we would take up the kite-flying and the mischief, from where we would have left off, the moment he returned home for the holidays.'

Film songs and classical ragas, Mohammad Rafi's songs, the Gurbani with its deep piousness—these would form the alphabet of Jagjit's musical vocabulary. His love for music now ran deep, pulling him to listen, whenever he got the chance, to eminent singers at concerts not just in his town but wherever there was a performance nearby. Sometimes he would get so immersed in a song, or in listening to the music playing somewhere, that he would forget the errand he had been sent on, and return only when the spell released him, often to face his father's anger. He was an obedient boy though, and never answered back, or even tried to explain himself. But the habit of drifting away into his musical world never left him.

Slowly, his voice too found itself, giving him a certain reputation as a singer of some accomplishment. Little wonder then, that in the processions that wound their way through the streets, and in the Gurdwara, Jagjit's voice would often

Parents, Amar Singh and Beeji

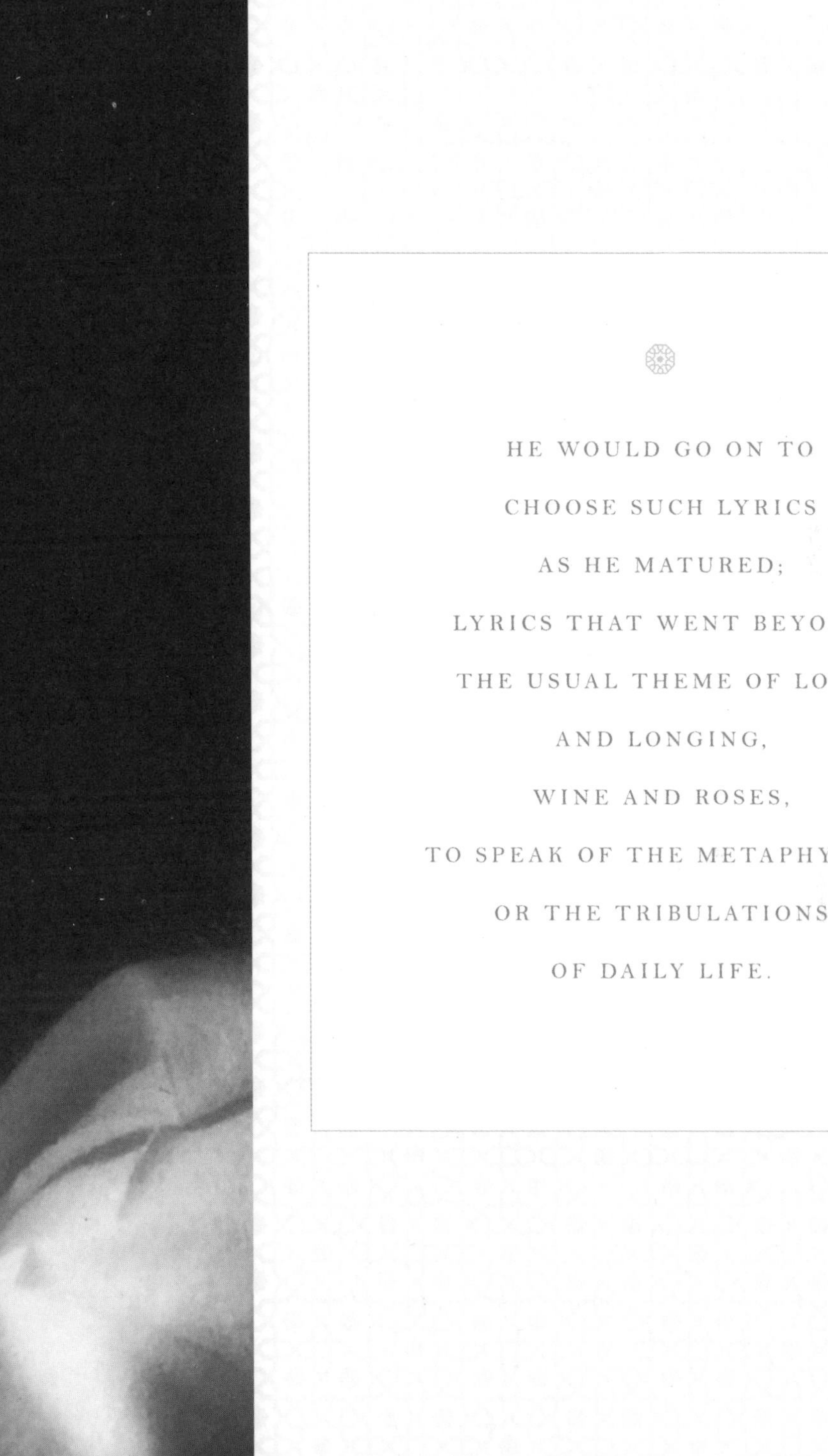

HE WOULD GO ON TO
CHOOSE SUCH LYRICS
AS HE MATURED;
LYRICS THAT WENT BEYOND
THE USUAL THEME OF LOVE
AND LONGING,
WINE AND ROSES,
TO SPEAK OF THE METAPHYSICS
OR THE TRIBULATIONS
OF DAILY LIFE.

be chosen to lead one of the groups that sang the shabads.

It was when he was in class nine that Jagjit Singh first tasted the success that would flood his music in the years to come.

With customary seriousness, he prepared diligently for the occasion—a Kavi Darbar, where singers would sing on themes related to the Gurus or on contemporary issues. 'We used to get a Namdhari magazine at home called *Satyug*, in which I read a geet I liked so much, I copied it. *"Ki tera aitbaar o rahiya"*,' Jagjit said referring to the song he sang at the Kavi Darbar.

It was a philosophical song, melancholy and haunting. Already, the young singer's choice was being shaped. He would go on to choose such lyrics as he matured; lyrics that went beyond the usual theme of love and longing, wine and roses, to speak of metaphysics or the tribulations of daily life.

Making bold to set the lyrics to a tune, he based his song on Raga Bhairavi. The first milestone of creativity was thus laid. Now it remained for the audience to decide what they thought of it. Their decision would change the course of Jagjit's life.

As it transpired, the young singer held his own, inspiring a shower of coins on to the stage even as he sang his raga. When the cries for an encore resounded, he took recourse to his love of film music and sang one of his favourites, again a melancholy number, *'O duniya ke rakhwale'*, from *Baiju Bawra* and sung by Rafi. Predictably, with this extremely popular number, Jagjit Singh brought the house down.

Movies were becoming a passion. He would sneak off to see films like *Nagin* and *Shirin Farhad*, not once but many times over, because they had songs that thrilled his heart. 'Of course, there was no question of asking Father for money. So what we would do is gather bits and pieces of discarded tickets, sort them out, and see which ones we could match and stick together to make a whole ticket. Then we would wait for the most crowded time to press in. Or we would wait for the movie to begin and give a sympathetic gatekeeper a couple of annas to let us in. But my father always found out. I don't know how. Once, I was seeing a movie when I was collared by Father and taken home on his bicycle,' Jagjit said, recollecting those days.

Kartar has memories of the pantomime that would be played out each time a new film came to town. 'He was particularly fond of

Shammi Kapoor. We were all huge fans, in fact. When he was able to arrange tickets, he would signal to us to get ready. We would change into shorts and shirts, and sit in the front of his bike on the crossbar. My cousin and I were the ones he pampered this way. He would put us in the front seats in the cinema hall and disappear. When the movie ended, he would be there to pick us up. It was so exciting.'

If singer Kishore Kumar copied K. L. Saigal before he discovered his own style, Rafi was Jagjit's idol. In soiree after soiree, he would sing Rafi's popular numbers, choosing the ones that tore at the heartstrings. At a college function, by which time his reputation as a singer had grown considerably, he regaled a crowd of almost 4000 people with his rendition of *'Yeh duniya agar mil bhi jaye to kya hai'* from *Pyaasa.* Even when, to everyone's dismay, the power failed and the lights went off, the singer could not be separated from his song. He kept singing. Luckily, the battery-operated sound system continued to function and the audience listened, entranced.

Knowing now where his future lay, Jagjit Singh decided to place all his faith in his abilities as an artiste. Like others who worship at the altar of music, demanding as it is, he had to take firm decisions and make difficult choices. Though a skilled hockey player, he pulled out of the college team to save himself for the ruling passion of his life.

It was a wise choice. The goddess of music would soon express pleasure over his sacrifice.

2

Saraswati is a gentle goddess. Her personification as a woman seated on a lotus over soft waves, which hardly ripple the still of the waters they rest on, and the fact that she is dressed in white and gold, are suggestions of her benign nature. The veena she holds in her hands is a harmonious instrument; even when played at a great tempo, its sound is never loud or jarring. Known to bestow largesse on those who worship at her altar, Saraswati can bless a devotee with wisdom and the gift of expression through words or music. Yet even this gentle goddess demands some proof of commitment and devotion before adding to her gifts the blessing of success.

Jagjit Singh too would walk the tough road. But, for now, she was still leading her devotee by the hand, guiding his talent towards fruition.

The radio was still his best friend. The songs it played through the day would vary. From film music to the classical, from thumris to ghazals. Something about the ghazal must have caught Jagjit's attention. The way the words leaned on the tune and the manner in which the tune supported the words. Together, they created, in the ghazal, a gem of exquisite beauty, capable of touching the listener's heart.

He still daydreamed in class, there was little room in his life for learning by rote. But the words of the ghazals, the power they could wield over the listener, made a deep impression on him. Words would always hold prime position in his songs, adding to the mood of the compositions that were to spin forth from him in the future.

His familiarity with great names came second-hand, over the air waves. But like Eklavya, drinking deep from the fount of Dronacharya, Jagjit would listen to the likes of Bade Ghulam Ali Khan and Amir Khan on the radio, and take from them lessons that he would blend into his own style. Anil Biswas had, by then, polished the soft brilliance of a ghazal singer named Talat Mahmood, and his songs, filmed on the icons Dilip Kumar or Dev Anand, had captured the imagination of our nation. Jagjit Singh, too, still shaping his own voice and talent, found himself listening greedily to the ghazals that Talat crooned. Not surprisingly, he would feel the same attraction for the lilting melodies that composer Madan Mohan created, indulging in his partiality towards the ghazal.

If he had any doubt that he was on the right track, it was wiped away when he was selected to represent his college at the national-level Youth Festival in Delhi. 'I first took part in the Inter-Collegiate Youth Festival,' Jagjit Singh said, recollecting the process of selection that finally saw him on a national stage. 'First you had to compete within the state, which I did at Pilani, where I tied with another boy for the first place in classical music. So we both went to Jaipur where I sang Raga Adana and was chosen to represent what was then Rajputana University at the festival in Delhi.

'It was grand. For a full seven days, we were all camped at Talkatora Gardens in Delhi, about five or six thousand students from all over India. During the day, there would be theatre and music, and at night campfire and singing.'

The young singer was coming into his own, interacting with others who were possibly as talented as himself. His interactions with the arts that were related to music, like drama and dance, must have had a deep impact on him. Perhaps, the seeds of the warm and easy manner with which he would charm his fans from the stage in the later years were sown here.

Jagjit rubbed shoulders with many other artistes, some of whom were as passionate as him. Among them, Amjad Khan who had come as part of a Bombay theatre group, singer Purushottam Lal, who was representing Punjab, and Subhash Ghai, with whom he would forge a friendship that lasted his entire life.

'I used to grab the gold medal in dramatics, he would win his for classical music,' the producer-director said. 'It was a portent of things to come.'

Ghai and Jagjit continued to meet at other inter-state festivals. Himself a singer of some talent, Subhash Ghai would join his new friend as they sat together at night, sometimes by themselves, at other times by the campfire, and sing together the songs they knew.

It was at one such festival that Subhash Ghai suddenly realized the full measure of his friend's talent. 'We were at an inter-university competition in Bangalore,' he recalled. 'Though it was 11 p.m., there was no stopping the event as it rolled on. One student after another came up to the mike and sang fantastically. South Indian singers are so well trained, they have amazing confidence and expertise. The audience was equally charged, applauding each performer with great enthusiasm. Then it was Jagjit's turn. When it was announced that the student from Punjab University was presenting a classical number,

Jagjit performing at a college function before the then Lok Sabha Speaker, Dr Gurdial Singh Dhillon

SLOWLY THE MAGIC UNFOLDED.
THE CROWD GREW SILENT, THE AUDIENCE STARTED LISTENING. IT WAS AN AUDIENCE THAT UNDERSTOOD CLASSICAL MUSIC WELL.
SOON, THEY WERE CLAPPING, FIRST TENTATIVELY AS IF TAKEN BY SURPRISE, THEN ENTHUSIASTICALLY, ALMOST EVERY FIVE SECONDS. WHEN JAGJIT ENDED HIS SONG,
THEY CLAPPED FOR SO LONG AND SO LOUDLY THAT WE WERE IN TEARS.

there was a bout of laughter from the audience. It implied that Punjab was better known for the folksy Bhangra numbers; why would a boy from Punjab want to take on the classical-loving South?

'Jagjit entered and took his place at the mike. Seeing a Sardar with a turban and beard, the audience burst into laughter again. There was a lot of commotion, with some boys whistling and shouting. Through it all, Jagjit stood for a long moment with a half-grin on his face. Then, he started his alaap, but the audience laughed louder. The noise was deafening. I remember thinking, "It's over, he is going to flop." But Jagjit held his ground. He continued singing, his voice flowing clear and pure, over the noise from the crowd. Slowly the magic unfolded. The crowd grew silent, the audience started listening. It was an audience that understood classical music well. Soon, they were clapping, first tentatively as if taken by surprise, then enthusiastically, almost every five seconds. When Jagjit ended his song, they clapped for so long and so loudly that we were in tears. He won the first prize.'

By this time, Jagjit had left Sri Ganganagar in search of better pastures. His aim was to find greater opportunities for his music to shine.

Among the vast collection of photographs that, fortunately, still

The DAV College winning team. Jagjit Singh with singer Purushottam Lal (centre) and sitar player Joginder Singh. Seated in front are Principal Suraj Bhan flanked by Prof. Tara on the right and Prof. Chaudhary on the left

exist is one that seems to have little to do with singing. A callow-faced, turbaned Jagjit stands besides two others, fellow students, behind an august line of seated personages, obviously teachers. The eye is caught by the eleven large shields that stand in the forefront of the picture. Though the subjects of the picture are clearly conscious of the camera and consequently look stiff and formal, a closer glimpse shows that the half smiles on some of the faces are not the artificial smiles people normally offer to the photographer, but ones that talk of ownership and successful endeavour.

In Suraj Bhan, the principal of DAV College in Jalandhar, which Jagjit Singh joined to study for a B.Sc. degree, he found a kindred spirit, who used his position to patronize the arts as much as he leveraged it to further the cause of education. Bhan would waive off the hotel and other fees for gifted students such as Jagjit, and thus drew to his institution enough talent to ensure that his cultural team shone at inter-collegiate events and competitions. It was not long before Jagjit was absolved of the need to pay fees to continue in college. As long as the trophies kept coming, fees did not matter. Jagjit was obviously among the stars of the cultural team of DAV College during his time there.

Of course, the pursuit of his musical interests left little time for studies, and led to some humorous situations too! Bestselling Hindi crime fiction writer, Surender Mohan Pathak, who was in the same college as Jagjit Singh, has many stories to share. 'DAV College, in those days, was on the outskirts of Jalandhar Township and the new hostel was across the road from the college. The hostel was a massive, double-storey, stand-alone, rectangular building with hundreds of rooms housing some seven hundred students. The occupant of one such room on the first floor, facing GT Road, was a handsome, strapping young Sikh from Ganganagar known as Jagjit Singh, pursuing his B.Sc. with me. So, we were not only hostelmates but also classmates.

'The jail-like hostel was such that some rooms were much sought after, while others were likened to prison cells by those housed in them. Naturally, every student was on the lookout for a comparatively better room. The management sorted this issue in an interesting manner: the student who secured the highest marks in the previous exam would have the first choice of the room, and so a kind of merit list was drawn. The most disadvantageous rooms that the tail-enders of the merit list had to contend for were on either side of the stairs, with ceaseless commotion, or on either side of the baths and toilets, and on either side of a boarder known as Jagjit Singh. This was because Jagjit Singh would practise his singing with a two-hour riyaz that started at five every morning when his neighbours were still fast asleep and were generally awakened by the loud, classical singing of "that godforsaken, inconsiderate third year science student".

'The riyaz session would be repeated for two hours, starting at five every evening. Due to the unending "ruckus", the boarders who lived adjoining Jagjit Singh's room considered themselves a persecuted lot.

'On other occasions too, he would catch hold of any fellow boarder in the corridor and sing a melodious film song for his benefit. Most often, the listener was anything but appreciative, and would shake him off, adding, *"Yaar, tu ne toh pass hona nahin, humein to padhne de."* To this, Jagjit Singh would retaliate angrily, "*Saalon,* you will not listen to me now, but there will come a day when you'll pay for this privilege." Such was the self-confidence of the would-be music maestro when he was just 19 or 20.'

In fact, Jagjit was so fond of performing for an audience, he would take the most audacious chances to find himself a listenership. Principal Suraj Bhan would often speak to the students over the public address system. He would then go home for lunch. 'For the remaining twenty-five minutes, Jagjit Singh would station himself with his harmonium before the mike in the principal's office and sing to his heart's content. There was no way he could see from the room whether anyone was listening, but he sang nonetheless, and was almost certain that he had an appreciative audience among his peers. But that was hardly the case,' Pathak recollects.

Working to further the exposure to his talent, Jagjit also auditioned for the local All India Radio station. In the inscrutable manner in which the examiners at auditions take decisions, AIR's examiners failed Jagjit Singh in the light music category but passed him in the classical category, granting him the status of a 'B-class' artiste. This gave him the chance to sing six times a year, and in a live programme for a duration of fifteen minutes. 'The money I earned came in handy, but more than that, it was the exposure I was getting and the learning process that kept me knocking on the doors of the radio,' in Jagjit's own words. His diligence paid off as he was soon given approval to perform in the light music category too. His voice was now heard over the air waves singing lighter songs.

It was beginning to be heard more appreciatively in his own college too. Lohri was a festival which was celebrated only in Punjab. On the night of the festival, there was a celebration for all the boarders and a stage show was organized by the college management. Many artistes, mainly from All India Radio, Jalandhar, participated and, in the music section, the only local talent, the lone college participant was the irrepressible Jagjit Singh. He would wait patiently till all the big names had sung and, more often than not, by the time his turn came, the young audience would have had enough. Yet, the students would want him to take his chance at the mike, and he would gladly do so.

Outside the 'disadvantageous' rooms

Pathak remembers, 'While in college, we celebrated Lohri thrice, and each time, Jagjit Singh sang the same song at the audience's insistence, and there never was a dry eye left. Many students would openly sob and the spell would not be broken even when the song was over. The song was "*Ay taa jag diyaan lohriyaa, saadhi ka di lohri akkhaan sajnaa ke modiyaan*".'

Alongside his radio recitals, he also began to sing by invitation, at private parties, where a pleased host or listener would sometimes lovingly press a hundred-rupee note into his hand.

Slowly and gently, Jagjit was being guided towards his destiny.

JAGJIT PLAYING ACCOMPANIST ON THE HARMONIUM AT A COLLEGE CON

Not everybody who looks back on his life can see the milestones clearly. The twists and turns life takes, the sudden highs and unpredicted false turnings obscure one's view and confuse the mind. There are many instances of people who started out to be something, and after investing a lot in pursuing that line of life, changed tracks, willfully or due to accident or chance, to find success and fame in quite another space.

The milestones in Jagjit Singh's life, however, are clearly marked. They dot his passage to fame and success at regular intervals, and it seems that every milestone was planted by some guardian angel whose purpose in life was to guide the singer on his path.

Purushottam Lal too can be counted among his guardian angels, for he changed Jagjit's life by merely studying in the same college as him. Classmate Surender Mohan Pathak remembers that Purushottam was an Arts student in DAV, but had also been a staff artist of All India Radio, Jalandhar since he was eight years old.

Both were classical singers. They had vied with each other earlier at the International Youth Festival. Each admired the other, and yet there was enough ground for rivalry. Only one of them could represent the college at inter-college musical competitions, and that was enough cause for concern.

The manner in which Jagjit Singh approached and solved this dilemma is indicative of his approach to life in his later years. Never one to seek out trouble or take on the role of the aggressor, young Jagjit decided that since he could sing light music just as well as classical ragas, he would compete in the light music category. The idea won him laurels, apart from the friendship of his 'rival', with whom he later collaborated on college competitions.

'Now the college had a strong team: Lal for classical, myself for light, and a sitar player whom we had taken from radio and enrolled in college for instrumental: these were the three types of entries. We entered many compositions and won trophy after trophy. Other teams would see us coming and say, "*Mar gaye*, we are dead!"'

Of course, there was almost no time to study, even if one wanted to. Jagjit neither attended lectures nor paid any attention to his books. Even the practical classes in science were but ways of proving his virtuosity in music. Pathak remembers an incident: 'In the Physics lab, we had to experiment on how resonance

Singing for the President of India. Also seen on dais from right to left: Dr Rajendra Prasad, President of India, Suraj Bhan, and Pratap Singh Kairon, CM of Undivided Punjab

could be achieved. The experiment required two taut, stretched, piano wires to resonate at the same frequency. For this, a tuning fork was required. We would use it to create resonance in one wire and then bring the second wire on the same frequency.

'Jagjit Singh always accomplished this without the help of the tuning fork. He, then, would invite the instructor to check his experiment, and the instructor would exclaim, "Jagjit, did you not get the tuning fork issued for the experiment?" And Jagjit's answer would be, "*Mainu nahin pata*. You check whether it is correctly done or not!" And, to the great surprise of the instructor, he always found it done perfectly, as Jagjit Singh's ear was naturally tuned to the intricacies of sound.'

But his talent for music was not of any help in academics. And when the time for exams came, Jagjit realized there was nothing worthwhile in his canvas of knowledge that he could transfer on to the exam sheets. He bunked the exams, and switched to Arts to repeat the third year. Student life, with its chances of shining at competitions, suited him well indeed, as long as he did not have to focus on studies.

Happy coincidences continued to occur throughout Jagjit Singh's life as a student. And he was able to recognize and seize the opportunity when it came by. One such came with the impending visit of the then president of India, Dr Rajendra Prasad. The year was 1962. Jagjit Singh, by then acknowledged as an accomplished singer and winner of medals, was the obvious choice to sing the welcome song.

Not content with singing a shloka or a routine welcome song, Jagjit decided to create something special. Approaching his acquaintance who worked at All India Radio at the time, he asked him for a poem for the occasion. The writer obliged, and Jagjit Singh set it to music.

Though neither of them knew it then, the writer of the poem, Sudarshan Faakir, would scale the heights of fame later on and be known far and wide as a poet, and throughout his career in music, Jagjit Singh would mine Faakir's writings and set them to his tunes.

When Dr Rajendra Prasad took the stage during his visit to the college, Jagjit sang the song that Faakir had written: *'Swagatam, swagatam, kehte hain hum apne mehman ko pranaam...'*

Indicative of another aspect of Jagjit's nature was the remuneration received by Faakir. 'He got me a sum of Rs 300, unheard of in those days when poets writing for the radio got Rs 25 for five ghazals,' Faakir remembers.*

Sudarshan Faakir was not the only significant person to cross Jagjit Singh's path in the early '60s. Other well-known personalities played their part in steering the singer towards his goal, often without realizing that they were doing so. Among them was the character actor, Om Prakash.

Jagjit Singh also found a place in the handpicked cultural team that Punjab's well-known police chief, Ashwini Kumar, put together to represent the state at the National Police Cultural Meets. So adept was Ashwini Kumar at selecting the best that he managed to win most of the trophies for his state at the Meets, year after year. At one such event held in Shimla, Om Prakash, who was shooting for a film there, held a mehfil at his place where he invited Jagjit to sing. Impressed by Jagjit's talent, he told the singer to try his luck in films. In fact, he offered to help should Jagjit ever come to Bombay. A year later, Jagjit decided to take a chance. En route from Ooty, where he had gone to yet another Police Cultural Meet, he stopped by in Bombay.

**The quote has been taken from the book* Beyond Time, *a limited edition published by Pankaj Kodesia & Associates in 2002*

THE STAR OF THE CULTURAL TEAM

'So I came to Bombay and stayed in a small hotel near the VT railway station, where every morning I would be woken up by what was then the latest film hit, "*Teri pyaari pyaari surat ko...*" playing at full volume. Om Prakash used to stay in Chembur and I contacted him there. He received me very warmly and introduced me to the famous music directors of the time, like Madan Mohan and Shankar-Jaikishen. I also met Jaidev and Manmohan Krishna, who ran a radio programme of ghazals. Jaikishen gave me a voice test at Famous Studio. He liked my voice but told me it would take time and that I would have to live in Bombay,' remembered Jagjit.

He had no inkling of it then, but the street Jagjit wished to enter bore a huge 'No Entry' sign.

THE NEW SINGER IN BOMBAY

4

It has happened to almost every seeker who comes to the 'City of Dreams', aspiring to become a part of the magical world of Hindi cinema. The pull of movies is great. The romance and the myths that are thrown at the big screen by the projector inside the darkened confines of a movie hall get reflected in the minds of all those who sit inside watching fictional lives unravel. Off-screen, the adulation and the fame with its perks of money and comfort that stars enjoy add an edge to the wanting. Almost every cinemagoer, at some time or the other, dreams of belonging to the Tinseltown where everything is larger than life, and where fact and fiction merge into an indistinguishable whole.

Yet, reality is a harsh blade that cuts into the psyche. Aspiring actors, singers, writers, poets, who among those, who have made cinematic history today, has not walked the streets, slept on pavements or waited with a slowly extinguishing hope outside a producer's door, thirsting to be noticed. Some strike gold, their talent gets a platform, others find a godfather who has made it his mission to nurture new talent. And some, by pure chance, get a break even though they were not expecting it. The rest, defeated and spent, languish on the fringes or slink away into some dim place where they can hardly remember who they were or discern what they have become. Yet, every day brings new dreamers into Bombay; they all come seeking their place in its sun.

Jagjit too had such dreams. And he felt they could indeed come true. The talent he was gifted with had now flowered, and brought with itself the scent of success and modest fame. If he could only transplant the flower into the garden of films, there would be no stopping him.

But he would soon find out that reality was not in step with his hopes.

The playback scene he wished to storm was a bastion that was practically impregnable. A star system existed that was as inviolate in the minds of the public as it was in the minds of those who made films. The triumvirate of Raj Kapoor, Dilip Kumar and Dev Anand ruled the silver screen through the '60s, though there were others who could also be called stars.

Each of the three had his 'voice', so to speak. A producer himself, Raj Kapoor had found in Mukesh a voice perfectly matching his own. And Dilip Kumar, himself gifted with musical knowledge had adopted Mohammed Rafi as his singing voice. Dev Anand swung between Rafi and Kishore Kumar. The lesser stars had their own voices too. Rafi with his surefire saleability, unerring sense of melody, his knack of adapting his voice to the actors' vocal mannerisms and characteristics was the producers' choice for most of the others, from Jubilee star Rajendra Kumar to comedian Johnny Walker and all those in between. And then there were Manna Dey and Hemant Kumar among those vying for music directors' attention.

But Jagjit had come from far off Jalandhar and his naiveté kept him from seeing beneath the surface. When, in the kindness of spirit, music director Jaikishen told him he could give him a chance but it could mean a long wait, Jagjit could not have understood the ramifications of that statement. Even a star musician like Jaikishen would have to endeavour to find a chink in the system to be able to help Jagjit become a playback singer.

Ignorance was bliss. Happy that some hope had been offered, but knowing he could not last without money or friends in the city any longer, Jagjit took a train back home. By now he was practically penniless, and had to hide in the toilet each time the ticket collector came around to check tickets, because he had none and lacked the wherewithal to buy one.

Putting off his plan of becoming a playback singer for the time being, Jagjit Singh set about fulfilling his filial duties. Amar Singh wanted this gifted son of his to enter the civil services, and Jagjit Singh dutifully obliged. To this end, he ensured he passed the college final exams, studying at the last minute for some subjects, and copying unabashedly from notes that were shared with other equally clueless classmates for the subjects that they had ignored. 'In the history exam, we sat next to each other and passed the answers around, taking turns with each question. The invigilator turned a blind eye, perhaps because I had sung shabads at his house, but other eyes were watching. Somebody reported us to the Inspector.

'The next day we were confident we would get away with it again; we had come fully loaded with chits. An hour after the paper began, the Inspector came and, with a grave face, called us out of the room. We thought we were going to get some severe punishment. Instead, he seated us in the next room, which was empty, and said, "Copy here in peace, others will complain if you do it there."'

Once the results declared that Jagjit Singh had passed, his family moved to Ludhiana. Amar Singh had retired and bought a small piece of land where he hoped to set up a small factory to keep himself busy. The move proved lucky for Jagjit too. Despite his getting a third class in his exams, he managed a seat in the local college for further studies. As luck would have it, his old principal, Suraj Bhan, had just taken over as vice-chancellor of the newly-instated Kurukshetra University. Still garnering his dream and pursuing his love for music, Jagjit laced his evenings at the college hostel with singing to the accompaniment of the tabla played by Iqbal Singh, a friend whom he had persuaded to join the same institution and shared a room with.

Life in the college took on the same tenor as his earlier collegiate days. Little study and plenty of fun, and music at every turn. He had no idea as to how he was going to get through the exams when the time came; he knew what he wanted most was to sing for films. Others among his friends were of the view that he would never make a good civil servant. His passion was music, and they encouraged him to pursue it. Among the most vocal was Hardman Singh Bhogal, dealer in cycle parts and a close friend of both Jagjit and his family. 'Bhogal told me he would help me, and after assessing my capabilities, I had the feeling I could make it too,' recalled Jagjit.

Bhogal kept his word, and soon, without a word to anybody, not even his dearest brother Kartar Singh, Jagjit Singh was boarding the train to Bombay once again. The hope he held close to his heart, that he would make good, would come true in ways he could never imagine.

Aayen hain samajhaane log
Hain kitne deewaane log

Dair-o-haram mein chain jo milta
Kyun jaate maikhaane log

Jaan ke sab kuchh kuchh bhi na jaane
Hain kitne anjaane log

Waqt pe kaam nahin aate hain
Ye jaane pehchaane log

Ab jab mujhko hosh nahin hai
Aayen hain samjhaane log

BOMBAY DREAMS

The Victoria Terminus Station in Bombay is a landmark for tourists. Declared a World Heritage building by UNESCO, its mind-boggling mix of Gothic and Indo-Saracenic architechture has visitors and the occasional local standing in awe as they take in the leaping gargoyles and the perfect dome with the statue atop it. Today, Bombay has become Mumbai, and other rail hubs have been developed for outstation trains to terminate at.

But in 1965, when Jagjit Singh stepped out of the Pathankot Express as it steamed into the terminus, he must have, like a million others before him, been overwhelmed by the immensity of the place, as much as by the crowds that thronged the platforms.

The young man, however, was by now familiar with the city. Preferring comparatively cheaper and quieter lodgings to his earlier hotel near VT, he found a small room in Gope House near the Elphinstone Road station. Within days, his easy camaraderie and friendliness won him a small circle of friends. But life is never easy in any city for a newcomer with slender financial means. And Bombay is a relentless, cruel metropolis that keeps her own beat, rejecting those who cannot keep step with it, and rewarding a few who manage to accept her demanding ways.

Jagjit found himself adrift in no time. Thrown out of the tiny room at Elphinstone Road, he found accommodation in the Sher-e-Punjab hostel in Agripada for thirty rupees a month. It was crowded and dirty, and a far cry from the clean and meticulously run home his parents kept, or even the college hostels he had inhabited; but he had little choice. Moreover, his entire concentration was on making it as a singer. This then, he thought, must be just a rite of passage. He took it in his stride, even joking wryly about the bed bugs who grew plump and shiny feeding off the floating population who occupied the four cots in the room, and the fact that one night a rat took a bite off his heel. A small joy lay in the fact that the room was blessed with 'room service'. A teashop stood just below it, which he could call down to for bed tea.

Still chasing his dream, Jagjit would take the local train as it rattled emptily in the evening towards Churchgate where it would load on the working millions heading back to their suburban homes. At Churchgate, he would meet like-minded seekers of the stardust and while away the evening. Among them was his old friend, Subhash Ghai.

'We came with different dreams,' Subhash Ghai says, of those days of waiting. 'I hoped to be a hero, he wanted to sing playback in the movies. That was in the late 1960s. Mukesh, Rafi were all at the top, even Kishore Kumar who had been singing for years had yet to find himself on par with them. There was little room for a newcomer. I asked him, "Why playback?" He retorted, "Why hero!" I think we both laughed, though our hearts were heavy with no sight of a breakthrough.

'We would meet in front of Gaylords. So many of us hopefuls. We would walk the stretch of the pavement, stop for tea at Asiatic, which was a restaurant at the time. Then we would walk to the promenade and stroll by the sea. Sometimes we would spot a celebrity at Gaylords. It was a popular haunt for people from the industry. Jaikishen would often come there; Jaidev too. The place attracted all kinds of genteel people, who would sit in the semi-covered area sipping ice-cream floats and cold coffee from tall, slender glasses and eating chicken patties. They had the power to make dreams come true, but we seldom got a second look.'

Sometimes, the group would stop at Berry's on the same stretch of the road. Jagjit Singh acknowledges the kindness he received in those difficult days. 'Our patron and guide was Mr Berry, the owner of the restaurant. He used to allow me to eat there for free and was very helpful.'

Subhash Ghai would be among those watching his friend very carefully, tracing his graph as he moved towards finding his own space. 'Jagjit finally found a foothold in the city. He started performing at some music club functions, and at the annual gatherings of some clubs. He could be very funny, and his repertoire included bawdy Punjabi songs that he sang with gusto. Yet he had a gentle side that could seduce the listener. When in college, he would belt out the entire repertoire, including Saigal songs. I would join him in singing those, as I loved them too. Later, when he started singing ghazals, I was shocked! His style and quality were on par with Mehdi Hassan, at a level beyond imagination.'

Also in their group was another young man from Punjab. A fellow Sikh who hoped to spin music for the movies one day. Kuldeep Singh, who would later win acclaim for the music of *Saath Saath.*

Kuldeep has vivid memories of the time. 'I knew him as a fellow struggler. We were a few months

From left to right: Jagjit Singh with friends, Parikshit Sahni, Jadgish Raj and Sanjay Khan

apart in age. I was doing my M.A. in K.C. College at Churchgate, and we had our adda outside Gaylords every evening. We were a group of lost souls, who would stand outside and trade our day's experiences. I knew Jagjit Singh because at some point we had shared a stage at some function. We had got talking then, and a friendship developed. We had a common joke. I would tell him, "When I get my chance as a music director, will you sing for me?" And he would say, "Just let me get my chance in a film, and I will get you on board to make the music for it." I would stop for a paan sometimes, and if he happened to pass by, he would call out, "Where is my chance, when is it coming?" It was all talk in the air... the hopefulness of the hopeless.'

Their camaraderie involved keeping one another's morale high, and helping wherever they could.

Jagjit Singh was luckier than most. Jimmy Narula, who worked with HMV and often joined the group, arranged an audition for him.

Jagjit had been in the city for just six months when this break came.

Jagjit Singh forged enduring bonds with most of his musicians. Seen here at a rehearsal with Surinder Sharma (santoor), and Clarence Peterson (guitar) and Bhanwarlal (violin)

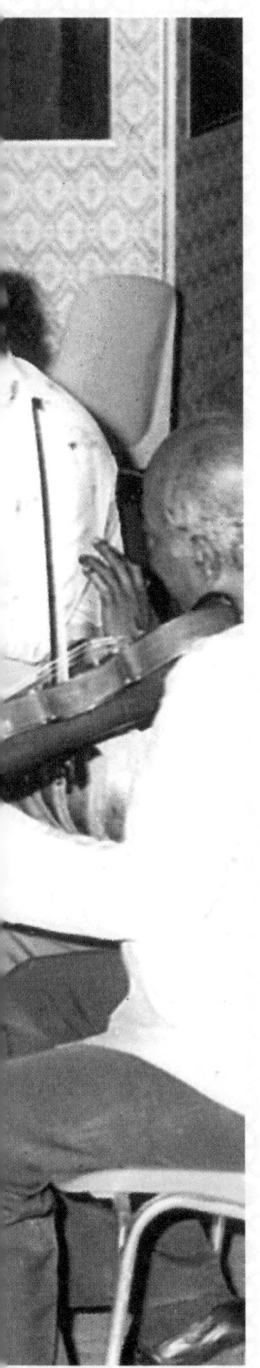

'HE STARTED PERFORMING AT SOME MUSIC CLUB FUNCTIONS, AND AT THE ANNUAL GATHERINGS OF SOME CLUBS. HE COULD BE VERY FUNNY, AND HIS REPERTOIRE INCLUDED BAWDY PUNJABI SONGS THAT HE SANG WITH GUSTO. YET HE HAD A GENTLE SIDE THAT COULD SEDUCE THE LISTENER.'

JAGJIT'S NEW PERSONA BEFORE HIS FIRST EP RELEASE

In a CD titled *Rare Gems* that traces the musical journey of Jagjit and Chitra Singh, there is a song that goes '*Saqiya hosh kahan tha*'. It follows another ghazal, '*Apna gham bhool gaye*'. Listen to both one after the other, and it is clear that in the space of that one recording, Jagjit Singh took a decision about his career. The two ghazals were on one side of the singer's first recording with HMV in the form of an EP or Extended Play. Two songs by another singer, Suresh Rajvanshi, made for the other side. Music for all the songs was composed by C.K. Chavhan. In '*Apna gham bhool gaye*', Jagjit adopted the style of Mukesh, who had given quite a few hit songs at the time and was top of the mind for fans, but did the second song in his own style. He was casting the dice and hoping to be accepted. In his mind, he must have prayed for the song in his own style to prove the more popular of the two.

The EP would add another twist to the flow of his life. Preparing for the release of the record, Jagjit took a sudden decision. 'I was told to take a picture of myself. I still had my long hair, my beard and turban. I decided to cut my hair. I knew then, whatever picture was taken, that was how I had to remain for the rest of my career, so I felt it was better to cut my hair. "Are you sure?" Asked the barber. "Yes," I replied.'

When he presented himself that evening to sing at a wedding reception, as he had been contracted to do, it took a lot of persuasion before he could convince the organizers that he was indeed the singer for the evening's entertainment.

The decision did wonders for his image, showing off his clean-cut features, bringing the focus to his lips when he enunciated his music, laden with meaningful words. But it almost put an end to his connection with his father, who did not brook this step that went against Namdhari Sikh tenets.

PERFORMING AT A PRIVATE PARTY

A seeker searching for a foothold in the slippery celluloid world has to be adaptable. He needs to rise to any occasion, don any garb demanded of him, and work quietly and assiduously towards using each demand made of him as an opportunity to climb out of anonymity.

In the pursuit of his career in films, Jagjit donned many roles. One such role was as a party extra in a film titled *Aman.* 'He played a sardar, with just one line of dialogue, but when the film was released in Ludhiana, a phone call came for us at a friend's house. Jagjit called to say he was arranging tickets for the film, we should go and watch. All of us went,' Kartar Singh recalls.

Jagjit did everything to keep afloat. He did small commercials. He sang at weddings, attended soirees at the homes of the rich and famous, where he would sing a few songs with no hope of remuneration besides a meal and the slim chance that his talent would be noticed where it mattered. He was tireless in his attempt to find that chink into which he could thrust the proof of his undeniable talent. But as time passed, Jagjit realized that the world of playback singing was not meant for him.

'The trouble is that even if someone is not seeking films, people push him into wanting it. There must have been countless people who must have told Jagjit, "You sing well, why don't you sing for films?"' said Gulzar, reminiscing about his first meetings with Jagjit Singh. 'Om Segan, a connoisseur of music, introduced me to Jagjit Singh. I used to live in the North Bombay Co-op Housing Society in those days. Om meant well. As I had worked with Bimal da, he thought I could wield some influence to help the singer. I, for one, everyone knows, had never wanted to be in films, *mera to accident ho gaya tha*, and that made me a songwriter, then one thing led to another. Om said, "*Iska bhi accident kara do.*"

'Om was a helpful type. Heavily into music, it was natural for him to come across fresh talent. He was the man who brought Reshma, the gypsy singer, to India. He got her tapes, and then her name just took off.

'Om brought Bhupinder along too. Jagjit and Bhupinder were both strugglers then. They sometimes shared a room, then they would get shunted out. Life was not easy. Both of them knew my younger brother in All India Radio in Delhi. It made me feel that they were like my younger brothers too. My feeling towards both of them was, "*Chota bhai aaya hai*", though, of course, I did not patronize them.

Enraptured audience around Jagjit Singh. From left to right: Raj Khosla, Ehsaan Khan (Dilip Kumar's brothe music director Roshan and Jagdish Raj. H.S. Rawail sits facing the singer.

'Jagjit sang for me. He sang "*Gulon mein rang bhare...*" I had heard it sung before by Mehdi Hassan, who was even then a big name. I was impressed by the way Jagjit sang the ghazal. He seemed to be of the same gharana as Mehdi, yet his rendition was different.

'His voice had a unique *dilasa dene wali* quality. It was like a half-healed wound, which you want to scratch because it itches, but hurts when you do so. It was a mix of pleasure and pain.'

If Gulzar felt the voice that impressed him was not suited to films, he said nothing about it. But the time would come when the two would find a common ground and forge a stronger creative bond.

With the first EP release, Jagjit felt he might finally find firmer footing. However, he would need to trust in his luck to make the most of his recording. There had been no publicity for the record's release. When he discovered that despite this, the record had sold 5000 copies, which was considered remarkable in those days, he had no idea whether it was his songs or the other singer's, which were responsible for the sales. And even if he did imagine it was him the public had liked, he wondered which of the two styles had pleased his listeners more.

He would get an answer soon enough. A call from HMV summoned him to the studio. The company wanted to record him again; he would get both sides of the next EP. 'I chose four songs and recorded them,' Jagjit said simply.

The rounds of celebrity homes continued, as did knocking on the doors of music directors. There was no other option, after all. In those days, there were only two ways to make a living out of singing. One was classical music, where singers would find an appreciative audience and be paid substantial amounts of money to sing to them. The second way, also guaranteed to bring fame and money to the singer, was the world of playback singing in films. Among the music directors Jagjit approached was someone whom he had admired hugely in his college days, and who shared his love for the ghazal—Madan Mohan.

'My father took kindly to Jagjit Singh. I was about ten or eleven when I first met him.' Sanjeev Kohli, Madan Mohan's son, has many memories linked to the singer. Chief among them is that first meeting, which held no hint of the fact that the boy and the man would forge an association that would span many years and result in some amazing music.

'My father used to go to a lot of posh parties; he was extremely popular, as were his songs. He would take his harmonium along, and an evening of singing and music would commence. One of his fans was Princess Usha Raje of Gwalior; there were many others, equally important and well-placed people.

'One evening, my parents were invited to one such party. It was raining heavily, I remember. My father told me, "An uncle will come. We are getting ready, make him sit. He will go with us." In a little while, the bell rang, and I opened the door. I saw a handsome, completely drenched man standing at the threshold. I could see that his chappal was broken. He looked very embarrassed about it. I made him sit. He told me he had recently come to Bombay, and met Madan Mohan-ji, who had encouraged him, and that he was accompanying him to a party.

'I knew he could not drag a broken slipper to a party. I went and fetched my father's favourite pair of

SHORT-HAIRED AND CLEAN-SHAVEN

Aligarhi sandals. Luckily, they fit him well. I asked to go along, and surprisingly, my parents agreed.

'The evening was a long one. The stranger, whom I was introduced to formally and whose name I learnt was Jagjit Singh, sang a few songs. My father, hoping to help him find ready listeners, had managed to fit him into the evening's programme. I was very young, but I noticed how he looked once he had finished singing. No one had paid much attention to him; he was a nobody after all, and that hurt him. I could see that. He said nothing though, and shyly retired to one corner of the room, and just sat there. I kept him company.

'Years later, when we became friends and worked together, he would joke about that evening. "I literally stepped into your father's shoes," he would laughingly say.'

The young Kohli would meet the singer again many years later, at an evening held in his father's memory. 'Lata-ji told me, "There is some new singer. Madan used to praise him. Why not ask him to sing too?" I contacted Jagjit; he had just recorded *The Unforgettables.* It was yet to be released. Jagjit Singh came to the event. He sang some of my father's compositions as well as some of his own. Lata-ji, Suraiya-ji and many others also took the stage that evening. Jagjit spoke of the gratitude and love he felt towards my father. And despite the fact that he was still struggling to find enough work, he did not charge a single rupee.'

Kohli did not know it then; perhaps neither did Jagjit. A few months after this evening, after the release of *The Unforgettables,* Jagjit would become a superstar.

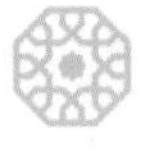

Ek na ek shama andhere mein jalaaye rakhiye
Subah hone ko hai maahol sajaaye rakhiye

Jinke haatho se hume zakhm-e-niha pahunchi hai
Wo bhee kehte hai ke zakhmo ko chhupaaye rakhiye

Kaun jane ke wo kis raah-guzar se guzre
Har guzar raah ko phoolon se sajaaye rakhiye

Daman-e-yaar ki zeenat na bane har aansu
Apni palko ke liye kuchh to bachaaye rakhiye

THE MAN IN WHITE PANTS

The Unforgettables, released in 1976, would catapult Jagjit Singh to an unprecedented level of popularity. Sharing the spotlight with him was Chitra Singh, life partner, singer and one-time student.

Chitra Singh was a married woman with a baby daughter when she first glimpsed Jagjit Singh from her balcony. She had no idea who this man was, but remembers noticing that he was wearing such tight white pants that it was a wonder he could walk. He had come to perform at the house of her neighbour.

At that time, Chitra was living in Baharistan, on Boman Petit Road, next to the Parsi General Hospital in South Bombay. Her neighbours were an older Gujarati couple. Having no children of their own, they had adopted an eight-month-old boy. The ayah would come to the balcony holding the baby in her arms, and Chitra would stand in hers, holding her daughter. Some silent communication developed.

The child would not drink his milk. One day, perhaps hoping that being with another child would make it easier, the maid took the baby and the glass of milk and knocked on Chitra's door. The idea worked. Within minutes, the glass was empty, and the children had become playmates.

When the boy's mother came to know about this, she came over to thank Chitra, and a friendship blossomed.

Though she had no inkling of the part he would play in her life, Chitra clearly remembers her first sight of Jagjit Singh. 'I could see a part of their drawing room from my balcony; I knew they often had musical parties. Both of them were fond of music, and would invite known and lesser known artistes for jalsas.

'I could not go across despite being invited. My daughter was still very young and would not sit quietly through an evening of music. But I would stand in the balcony and listen to the music as it floated across. One such evening, I saw a man come to the balcony for a smoke. He stood there, finished his cigarette and went back into the house.

'The next morning the lady called. "Do you want to listen to some music?" she asked, adding in appreciation, "*Kya gaata hai*, what a voice he has! Have you not heard of him?" she asked as I entered her house, "he is from Punjab."

'She put on the tape, and I listened to one song, then another. "Put it off. *Yeh bhi koi awaaz hai*!" I cried. She was flabbergasted. "You don't like him?" she asked, "He is quite popular. His name is Jagjit Singh."

PARTY EVENINGS: WAHEEDA REHMAN AND RAJ KHOSLA AMONG THE AUDIENCE

'"Is he a sardar?" I asked. "No," she said, "he is clean-shaven."

'"Well, I don't like his voice," I said, "Ghazals need to be sung like Talat Mahmood sings them." And I left.'

Chitra would not hear of or meet Jagjit for the next two years. Her husband, Deboo Prasad Dutta, was moving up the corporate ladder. As the branch manager of Britannia Biscuits, he was entitled to a company flat. The family moved to a more spacious home on Carmichael Road in South Bombay.

'Gulistan was a lovely building. We had a huge house on the top floor. It had a huge balcony too.'

When he was not at work, Dutta had a passion he indulged in seriously. Chitra remembers, 'He had a penchant for recording. He constantly checked out new advances in technology. In fact, he was the first to import quadrophonic recording equipment. He set up a four-channel recording studio in our drawing room and made full use of it. Not a day went past without somebody or the other coming in to record.

'Shyam Benegal, Dhanraj Bhatia, Mrinal Sen, they were all in and out, recording their songs. There was also one Mr Vaidyanathan. He wrote and recorded many radio commercials. Well, he was almost a permanent fixture there every single day.'

In his own way, this creator of jingles, Vaidyanathan, would prove to be an agent of Chitra's destiny.

She clearly remembers the day she first sang professionally. 'One afternoon, Vaidyanathan was at his wits' end. He had booked Lakshmi Shankar, Uday Shankar's sister-in-law for a recording, and she had not turned up. After walking up and down and wearing out my carpet, he approached my husband. Would I help him by singing the jingle? My husband said, "Ask her yourself." So he came and asked me.

'Of course I was scared. I had sung for Durga Puja functions in Calcutta, and on the radio, but that was a long time ago. "Can I do it?" I asked, half of myself. "Yes, of course you can," he said emphatically. So, I braced myself and sang the jingle.

'After that, he would not take anyone else. I lived in the house where the studio was; I was delivering the jingles the way they had to be sung, and soon I was recording in every conceivable language: Oriya, Telugu, Tamil, Nepalese. I must have sung in eighteen to nineteen languages. The copywriters would sit in the studio and correct the words or my diction. I soon earned the title, "Jingle Queen".'

Dutta's informal recording studio soon found more musicians coming over to use the high-end equipment to their advantage. Mahinderjit Singh, whose son Chinku Singh would gain fame as a guitarist later on, came over one evening. He had booked the studio to create a showcase recording of aspiring singers. Having heard from his brother-in-law, Govind Prasad Jaipurwala, about Chitra's singing, he wanted to listen to a recording.

Chitra says that when he heard it, he was bowled over and exclaimed, 'Why is she sitting at home?' He decided to include Chitra in the showcase he was recording that day. The others on the list included Manas Mukherjee, who would later be better known as Shaan's father,

Musical moments

Jaspal Singh of *Geet Gaata Chal* fame, and Sulakshana Pandit, among others, all of whom were waiting for a break as singers.

The aspirants started trickling in at 2.30 p.m. They started rehearsing. The bell would ring frequently and Chitra would, as the hostess, walk up to the door and let the visitor in. She remembers clearly the events of that afternoon. 'The bell rang again at 4.30 after most of the singers had already come in. I opened the door, and there stood a man, his arm on the doorframe, his head on his arm... fast asleep. He woke up with a start when the door opened.

'Mahinderjit looked up and said, "*Arre*, Lallu, *aaja*," and the man walked in, went to a corner of the carpet, lay down horizontally across its edge and fell fast asleep again. When the others had finished rehearsing, he was woken up. The cries of "*uttho uttho*" finally reached him through his slumber. He sat up, reached for the harmonium and, in a voice heavy with sleep, started singing.

'"When he finishes," Mahinderjit said, "He will sing one solo. Then you will sing a duet with him." I had recognized the voice and realized that this was the same man I had seen in very tight white pants in the balcony from my old house, whose recording I had not liked at all.

Every instrument bent to his command

'"I will not sing," I said emphatically. "I have a thin, reedy high-pitched voice, he has a bass voice. How can we sing together?"

'Jagjit looked at me when I said that. "Why do you need to sing?" he asked, looking around at the well-appointed house. His look implied that I was well-off, a married woman with a child, what need did I have to sing or earn a living from it. It totally put me off. I flatly refused to sing.'

So Jagjit Singh rehearsed his showcase song alone.

When Dutta came home for the recording, he listened to all the singers. 'He fell for Jagjit's voice like a ton of bricks,' Chitra recollects. 'For the next two days, he recorded him; then, it was done, and Jagjit walked out of our lives.'

CHITRA SINGH

Mahinderjit Singh was nothing if not a talent scout. He kept his eyes and ears open. The advertising industry needed new voices all the time, and finding them ensured his commission. Having heard Chitra sing, he found her enough assignments. As chance would have it, a year later, in 1967, Chitra found herself recording at the same studio as Jagjit. They finished their respective recordings and got talking. 'I asked him about himself. He said he had come from Punjab two years ago, and lived in a guesthouse in Agripada near Bombay Central. I offered him a lift because it was the decent thing to do. After all, we were in the same line. "I will get dropped first as Carmichael Road is on the way, then my driver will drop you off," I said. He agreed gratefully and got into the car.'

When they reached her house, Chitra invited the singer up for a cup of tea. He accepted. As he waited in the living room, she went into the kitchen to make the tea, as in her own words, 'It was not my style to have a full-time servant; my maid would come, clean up and leave.' As the water came to a boil, she could hear the harmonium that stood in the studio-cum-living room being played, and then Jagjit started to sing. He sat there singing by himself, and she sat and listened to him. Really listened, for the first time.

'He sang a ghazal, "*Dhuan uttha tha*". When he ended it, I asked him who it was by. "*Meri hai*, I've composed it," he said simply. I looked at him again. He was just twenty-five or twenty-six-years old at the most. I was impressed. More so because of the complete involvement with which he had been singing the song. He was one with it.

'He sounded completely different from the Jagjit Singh I had heard on tape. I think from that day I got hooked on his music.'

The man who gave Jagjit his first break: Chitra's first husband, Deboo Dutta

Not long after, Dutta returned. He was very pleased to see Jagjit. They spoke for a while, and when Jagjit Singh got up to leave, Dutta told him, 'You live alone, it must be lonely for you. Come over whenever you want.'

The young man took the invitation seriously. He would visit the Duttas every Sunday. 'I'd cook, he would come over and eat, then, sometimes if it got late, I would drop him home. A friendship developed.'

In fact, the Duttas held an open house every Sunday. A music group would gather in the mornings: Robin Chatterjee, chief recordist at Film Centre, other singers and Jagjit Singh. They would play carom, cards, and discuss music. Then, by early evening, they would drift away. Dutta would prevail upon Jagjit to stay and leave after dinner, because he lived alone. He was almost like a member of the family—everybody liked him. 'He was shy and quiet, and his talent for singing made him welcome in the small circle. My daughter, Monica, addressed him as Jagjit Kaku,' says Chitra.

Through that year and the next, Dutta kept Jagjit quite busy. He recorded not just jingles for Vaidyanathan at the Dutta home-studio, but also created music for ad films and documentaries. The two men shared a camaraderie that gave an impetus to their creativity.

The Dancer

Despite appearances, all was not well in the Dutta household. The marriage was not going smooth. It spanned not just an age difference but differences in outlook and maturity. The beautiful Dutta home hid cracks behind its calm facade. More than once, Dutta had told his wife that there was a gap between them that seemed unbridgeable.

Chitra had grown up a much-loved only child. Protected by her mother, she was never allowed anywhere alone, or made to do any work at home. Singing came naturally to her. She would hear a song and remember and reproduce it exactly, and she loved dancing. When he saw her for the first time, performing in a Tagore dance drama, Deboo Dutta, older, worldlier, and a man of the world, was instantly smitten. He immediately told his parents he had met the girl he wanted to marry. There was only one hitch. The bride-to-be was only fourteen. But Chitra was in college by then. A good student, she had completed her schooling early, thanks to a series of double promotions. When Dutta's parents went across with the proposal, Chitra's parents had no objection to an engagement. The marriage could be solemnized a few years later, they thought.

But Dutta was an impatient lover. He wanted to carry off his bride. Much coaxing and discussion followed and, keeping in mind the boy's good family, his job status and other considerations that parents of girls take seriously, the wedding took place ahead of schedule. Chitra was all of sixteen then.

She is frank in her telling of the story. 'When we came to Bombay on a transfer two years later, I was eighteen. He was a suave, corporate man, successful and well read. We were completely mismatched, but we were happy enough not to realize this.

'When Monica was born, I tried to be a good mother, and thought I was a good wife too. I had no idea things were not going right, that he found me wanting. Even when one day, he perfunctorily told me, "I know you like singing and are a good singer, so look for prospects. I will help you where I can. But finally, I would like to make my own life and move on..." I did not really understand what he was trying to imply. The significance of his words did not sink in. I had no exposure to the world, had no concept of a divorce. I promptly forgot about it.

'One day he came home with a woman, whom he introduced as his secretary. She had tea, was taken through the house to look around, and left. I took it at face value, till soon after, he told me he was interested in her and wanted to marry her—and that he would like a divorce!'

After that, Chitra lived with the knowledge that her husband was involved with another woman. Worse still, she was aware her daughter might also know of it. Her foremost thought was to protect the child from the pain she must feel in knowing that she might have to choose between her parents.

Sometime in 1968, Deboo Dutta came home with a lawyer. The '*kala coat wallah*' murmured that he did not want any tea, and motioned for Chitra to sit beside him on the sofa. He pulled out a sheaf of papers and asked her to sign. Only her high self-respect prevented Chitra from showing her shock and dismay when she realized that they were divorce papers. 'Nothing could let me belittle myself in anybody's eyes, I had such an inflated sense of self-respect even then. I looked the lawyer in the eye, looked at Dutta, and put out my hand. "Give me the papers," I said and, taking them, signed.'

This was the beginning of a strange phase in Chitra's life. Dutta was nothing if not considerate. With maturity and foresight, he arranged for Chitra in such a way that she continued to pursue her music, rehearse, and meet those connected with her singing assignments in the house she had shared with him. However, he got another place for the mother and daughter to sleep in at night, so that the divorce could proceed smoothly.

Chitra Singh remembers the first glimpse of what her new life was going to be like with amazing clarity. 'My earlier homes had been huge: two or three bedrooms, balconies, three or more servants, a car and driver. Then he told me that I had to live on my own, and gave me the keys to the house where I was to go. He would pay the rent for as long as it was necessary. I was also given a car and a driver, so that I could go from one house to the other without worrying about transport, and also move about as I wished in the city.

'I had no concept at all of a one BHK, let alone a one-room flat. I had never even seen one. My daughter and I took the car and went to the address. We opened the door. It was sort of furnished. A sofa set, a small dining table with four chairs. There was a small balcony with sliding glass windows. We went inside; there was a passage and a bathroom on one side and a small room at the other end. We discovered it was the kitchen. All of 7.5 feet by 12 feet, with a window, and the door opened inwards! My daughter and I looked at each other. Without saying a word, we left.

'We moved in soon after. The earlier tenants had converted the kitchen into a bedroom, there were two beds fitted in there with difficulty. My daughter and I decided to keep the bedroom as it was; the kitchen was set up at one end of the passageway. And we managed somehow.'

The word 'divorce' was never mentioned before ten-year-old Monica, who adored her father. He was her hero and he did not want to break her heart. Dutta would come over for dinner on almost every evening that he was free. He explained to Monica that because she was growing up and the other house was full of people coming and going, this place was ideal for her privacy. But Monica must have got more than a whiff of the truth. She would insist on visiting her father, and could not have missed seeing the clothes that hung in what had been her mother's wardrobe. She must have realized that there was a woman in her father's life, and it was not her mother. Though she was seared by the fact, the child had no option but to accept it as well as the other changes in her life.

It was much more difficult for Chitra. 'Once the divorce came through, all the friends who used to come home cut me dead. They acted as if they did not even know me. Once I was at Cafe Galleria, and this man, who used to come home regularly and praise the food I cooked, just put his head down on seeing me and crossed the road. Suddenly it was as if I were a nobody, completely new to the city. I felt alone, abandoned. But I put up a brave front for Monica's sake.'

If there was one consolation, it was the fact that all through the rough years leading to Chitra's divorce, and after it, she had one constant friend. Steady as a star to guide her life, Jagjit Singh had entered it once again.

Agar ho inaayat, ae jaan-e-mohabbat
Bana dijiye inko qismat hamaari
Bahot khoobsurat hai aankhen tumhaari

Jo sab se juda hai woh andaaz ho tum
Chhupa tha jo dil mein wohi raaz ho tum
Tumhaari nazaakat bani jab se chaahat
Sukun ban gayi hai har ek beqaraari
Bahot khoobsurat hai aankhen tumhaari

Na the jab talak tum hamaari nazar mein
Na tha chaand shab mein, na suraj saher mein
Tumhaari ijaazat tumhaari hukumat
Ye saara gagan hai ye dharti hai saari
Bahot khoobsurat hai aankhen tumhaari

CHITRA SINGH

Through the pre-divorce period of Chitra's life, Jagjit and she often sang jingles together. By then, the difference in their voices, her 'thin, reedy, high-pitched voice' and his 'bass' had carved a middle path that worked for them both. Chitra lived on the money she earned from the recordings; she would be paid up to Rs 200 per jingle, a handsome sum in those days, which many other artistes could not command. Their friendship knit closer.

It soothed Dutta to know that Jagjit was around to look after Chitra. He was a caring soul, and she, in need of someone to trust and turn to, was grateful. They went to the movies together, ate out at times. He would potter around the house sometimes. 'If there was a bulb to be changed, I could depend on him to do it,' says Chitra.

One of the people who would act as a catalyst in the lives of both Jagjit and Chitra was a guitarist named Clarence Peterson. Peterson performed on stage, often organizing shows, in which he sang Mohammed Rafi's songs and also played on the guitar as an accompanist. He remembers Jagjit approaching him soon after he had finished a live show in the '60s. 'Jagjit came up to me and appreciated my skills on the guitar. He was young, smart and good-looking but wasn't famous yet. "Let's make some music together," he told me. I agreed.'*

The journey was far from smooth. In 1972, the group went to East Africa for an orchestra show, where it was hard for them to get Jagjit, a ghazal lover, to sing a film song: '*Mere sapnon ki rani kab aayegi tu*'. 'He would groove to the music, dance a little onstage, and he pulled it off well. But when the show got over, he protested. "*Tum log mujhse yeh kya gaane gawaa rahe ho yaar ... Ab se main sirf ghazlein hi gaaunga!*" That was his first and last tryst with film music on stage until he sang at the launch of the album *Close to My Heart* in 2003,' says Peterson.*

The Africa trip was also a turning point of sorts in the relationship between Jagjit and Chitra. Chitra was invited to the trip on her own merit, but, of course, she was already quite close to Jagjit, who might have added his recommendation too. However, the trip made it clear to Chitra at least that Jagjit was definitely more than just a friend in need. As she remembers, 'At the time we went to Africa, you can say our relationship grew into a romance or a strong friendship, whatever you may call it. It was very deep. I needed him at

**Inputs from* Pune Mirror

every step; he was like my security blanket in every way.'

Even at the height of his success, Singh remained well-grounded. 'Jagjit never let success go to his head, and treated his old friends just as well after he became famous. He always attributed his success to his friends and co-musicians,' says Peterson.*

Though people believed he was, by nature, a serious man, those close to him will tell you about his sparkling sense of humour. 'I broke a guitar string once during a live show, and at several shows afterwards, he would caution me: *"Yaar, sambhaal kar bajaana ... phir tod mat dena".'*

Peterson's eyes turn moist when he speaks of how the singer went out of his way to ensure that he had a roof over his head. 'When I got married in 1979, I was living in a rented house. Jagjit insisted that it was time I had my own. Without telling me, he found a house in Chembur and paid the booking amount. That's the house I live in today.'

It did not end at that. About five years ago, when Peterson was bed-ridden, Singh regularly called to check on him. One day, he quietly left Rs 20,000 in his wife's bag.

Peterson has lost count of the number of shows they did together. The last one was on 16 September 2011 at Worli's Nehru Centre. 'I was back on stage with Jagjit after recovering from my illness. He would fondly call me Pritam Singh instead of Peterson. That evening, Chitra-ji too had come, and he gleefully told her, *"Dekho Chitra, Pritam Singh aaya hai ... ab show mein jaan aa jaayegi".'*

Soon after the trip to East Africa, it was obvious to Jagjit that he had found his partner in life. One evening while Chitra was cooking, he knocked on her door. When it opened, he entered and sat down on a stool. His eyes were red, he had a cold coming on, perhaps a fever too. He was coughing. Perhaps the need for a caring hand had brought him to Chitra; after all, there is nothing more miserable for one living alone than falling sick. With the instinctive flair that women have for dealing with such problems, Chitra placed a huge pan of hot water in front of him and instructed him to inhale the steam. It would clear his head and ward off the impending cold. The dish on the stove demanded her immediate attention and she turned away to continue to cook.

'Suddenly I heard a voice saying, "I want to marry you." I said, "I am still married." "The divorce is coming through, no?" Jagjit said,

**Inputs from* Pune Mirror *and* Open magazine

adding, "I'll wait." Chitra kept quiet. But Jagjit continued to visit, unruffled by the lack of response.

He showed his devotion in many ways, even babysitting Monica if Chitra had to go anywhere on her own. He helped Chitra do up her house; a cupboard was fitted in, a wall unit added to the living room. His mind was obviously made up—she was the one with whom he would spend the rest of his life.

They got married in 1970. Jagjit's father would have been proud of the simplicity of the ceremony. Jagjit had waited long enough. Chitra had been on her own for two years, and the divorce had come through. Dutta had married too, and his new wife would bear him a daughter soon. Jagjit proposed again. This time Chitra accepted. Her mind was clear too; she 'needed him at every step'.

Loving and loved: Jagjit and Monica

Living, as he was, in a city so far away from his home and family, Jagjit instinctively sought an older person to ask for blessings. Almost naturally, he found himself meeting Dutta and requesting his permission to marry his ex-wife Chitra. It was a sign of the childlike simplicity of his heart. A quality that he never lost and which endeared Jagjit to so many who came across him, even after he attained an unparalleled status as a singer-composer.

'He told me he would ask Dutta for permission, *"kisi bade ko poochna chahiye",*' Chitra recollects. Dutta, of course, had no objection. In fact, he countered by asking what took Jagjit so long to decide. 'Jagjit, with characteristic calm, responded, "This is the right time".'

His mind next turned to Monica. Picking her up from the Villa Theresa School, which she attended, Jagjit and Chitra took her to Kwality restaurant. There, as she dug into the delights of a super large ice-cream sundae, Jagjit broke the news that he wanted to marry her mother.

Monica must have expected the news in her heart of hearts all along, perhaps dreading it too, but

HAPPILY MARRIED

Chitra and Jagjit with Jagjit's father, Amar Singh

she said nothing. Chitra looked at her anxiously. The girl was so ferociously devoted to her father that her reaction could not be positive. But in her own way, Monica loved Jagjit Kaku as well. She loved his voice and his singing. And anyway, she had no say in the matter. At least now, the agony of not knowing what the future held was over.

Money was an issue. And Jagjit was a simple man brought up to believe in simple ways. The marriage ceremony was in keeping with this. When a few of his friends came to know that Jagjit was getting married, they pitched in. The tabla player, Harish, who would often come over for rehearsals, suggested they go to the nearby temple. The priest there could get them married. Fellow singer Bhupinder pitched in with two flower garlands. A box of sweets, too, materialized from somewhere.

The simple ceremony took just about two minutes, cost all of thirty rupees, and sealed the destinies of two people who, as man and wife, were about to change the face of ghazal singing in India.

OFFICIALLY A COUPLE: JAGJIT AND CHITRA

Marriage did not change anything, except Jagjit and Chitra were now officially a couple. But money was still a problem. Jagjit continued to sing at various social dos, in people's homes, at functions. Five years in the city and he was still 'the new boy from Punjab'. Though the invitations to sing came from the very people who could give him the break he so desired as a playback singer, like H.S. Rawail, and Raj Kapoor, when they threw held lavish parties, he gained little from them. There was seldom any money, or very little of it, though he would get his dinner and drinks. Chitra still smarts over the fact that he would not put his foot down and talk money. 'He wanted to establish himself and did not wish to risk rejection over payments. He remained that way all through his life.'

Gradually, Chitra too started singing in public. It started with singer Manna Dey hearing her at a private family party. 'He liked what he heard and suggested my name for singing *"Vaishnava jana toh"*. He also recommended me to Jaidev.' Chitra sang the bhajan at a hall near Shivaji Park for a small private function.

Even before their wedding, Jagjit had started training Chitra to sing in his style. 'I started singing his songs in late 1969. When we started, he already knew my range, and how my voice would adapt. There was an issue with language though. Urdu was not my language, even Hindi was something I was not completely comfortable with. But I was a good learner. I would imitate his diction perfectly, even when I could not completely understand the words or the emotion.'

Thus, when invited to sing as a couple at the Rang Bhavan in Bombay in early 1970, Chitra went along. 'Brij Narain organized ghazal programmes, and invited us to sing at the yearly concert. Jagjit had performed there before, but it was practically my first public concert. I was understandably nervous, but I agreed anyway. There were many artistes singing that evening; some were seasoned, but the majority were newcomers.'

Among the songs they sang were the two that had been on Jagjit Singh's first Extended Play release, which still remained popular. 'After the show, someone stood waiting for us backstage. He introduced himself as G.N. Joshi from HMV. He was a connoisseur of music, perhaps a trained singer himself. I think he was the CEO then. After complimenting Jagjit, he turned to me. "I love your voice," he said,

Arriving at a duet

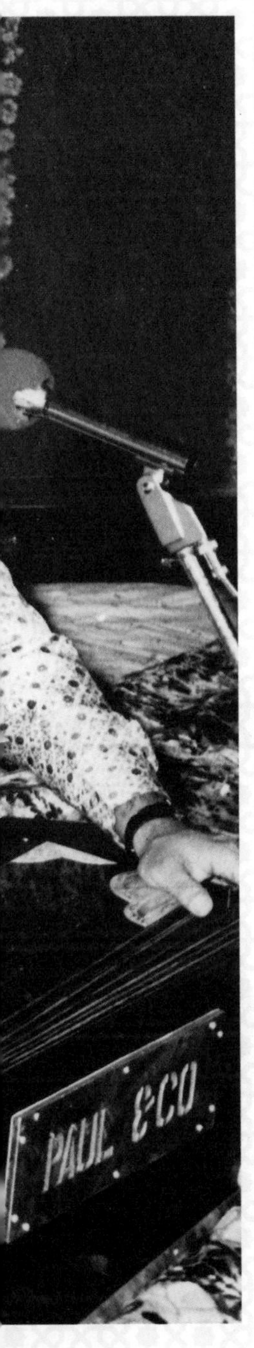

'I STARTED SINGING HIS SONGS IN LATE 1969. WHEN WE STARTED, HE ALREADY KNEW MY RANGE, AND HOW MY VOICE WOULD ADAPT. THERE WAS AN ISSUE WITH LANGUAGE THOUGH. URDU WAS NOT MY LANGUAGE, EVEN HINDI WAS SOMETHING I WAS NOT COMPLETELY COMFORTABLE WITH. BUT I WAS A GOOD LEARNER.'

smiling. "I retire in March and want to record your voice in December or January, because I don't know if my successor will follow my instructions."

'He gave us a date and we went to HMV,' Chitra remembers. Vice-president V.K. Dubey was there. He was a very enthusiastic man. "Let's find a famous director to create the music for you," he said. "Let's meet Khayyam."' Khayyam was already known as an offbeat composer for films by then. He was selective about his work, and most of the songs he composed went on to become hits and were praised for their melody.

Khayyam was indeed a well thought out choice. The composer had started an impressive track record of hits as far back as in 1958 with the Dilip Kumar-Meena Kumari starrer, *Footpath*, where his tuneful composition of *'Shaam-e-gham ki qasam'* sung by Talat Mahmood had won him instant recognition. He had followed it up with films that had increasingly well-loved numbers. *'Woh subah kabhi toh aayegi'* where his music combined with Sahir Ludhianvi's lyrics, and sung by Mukesh and Asha Bhosle, in a film, *Phir Subah Hogi*, with a powerful socialist message is still counted among the most powerful theme

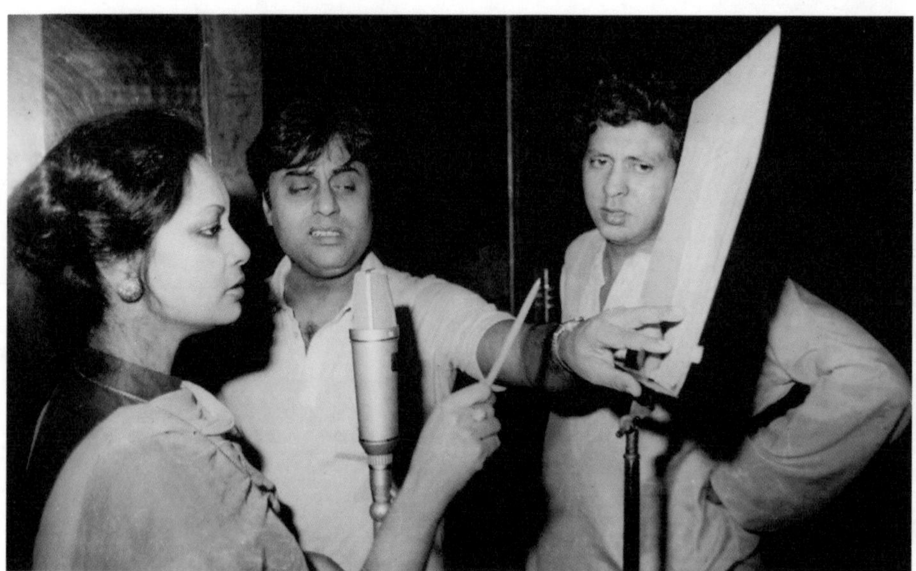

Raman Kumar, director of Saath Saath *watches as Jagjit rehearses with Chitra for a recording for the film*

songs in the history of film music. *Shagoon*(1964), *Khandan*(1965) and *Aakhri Khat*(1966) had cemented his reputation. But changing times and new entrants to the music field were also clamouring for attention. Perhaps that is why, post 1966 after *Aakhri Khat* was released, Khayyam had no projects in hand. Undeterred, the composer kept himself occupied. He composed for and released private albums, being almost the only composer of his time to do so.

Chitra and Jagjit met him at his place behind the Colaba post office in South Bombay. Chitra sang. The music director was pleased with what he heard. Chitra recalls that they also met his singer wife, Jagjit Kaur, and their son. Chitra and Jagjit were married by this time, and Monica would accompany them too. It was not long before, being like-minded music lovers, they got close as families.

'We made many, many trips to his house. There was plenty of talk on music, but no sign of recording any. Khayyam would say "very nice" when I sang, but no commitment came of it. Finally one evening, I asked nervously when we would start rehearsals. I was driven by the constant, nagging thought that Joshi would retire in March, and the months were galloping by. Khayyam replied, *"Arre, mujhe gaana gavana aata hai, recording ho jayega."*

'The next time I went, the same thing happened. There was no sign of a date for rehearsal or recording. I came to know there were singers of the stature of Asha Bhosle, who he had also been kept dangling. I had had enough of dinners that led nowhere. Their hospitality was wonderful, but I wanted it all to lead to what I was there for in the first place. Finally, I got fed up in true Bengali style. "This is leading nowhere," I told Joshi. "Let us forget Khayyam, his intentions are not clear." Which is when Joshi said, "Okay, let Jagjit compose."'

That was how Chitra Singh's first EP was created and released in January 1971. The four songs on it included '*Woh jo hum mein tum mein qarar tha*', '*Bas ke dushwar hai har kaam ka aasaan hona*', '*Yeh kiska tasavvur*' and '*Hamara bhi ek zamana tha*'.

In his element, working on the EP, Jagjit would compose and rehearse Chitra for each number before it was recorded at the HMV studio on Pherozeshah Mehta Road in the Fort area of South Bombay.

A streak of defiance that still burns in Chitra Singh, which often made her unpopular in an industry that demands a certain submissiveness

JAGJIT WITH JOHNNY BAKSHI(L) AND A FRIEND(R)

of women, prompted her to carry the first copy of her EP record in triumph to Khayyam. Jagjit was not comfortable with her mood, but he went along. 'Khayyam listened to the record, and as always we had dinner and were made to feel very welcome. Once the songs ended, he nodded and said, "achcha hai".'

Chitra also presented the record to Hridaynath Mangeshkar, who promptly played it on the radiogram. 'When the alaap of *'Bus ke dushwaar ...'* began, Lata Mangeshkar, who was elsewhere in the house, came running to ask who was singing.' Chitra still believes that though she appreciated Jagjit's voice and music, Lata Mangeshkar didn't feel the same way about her. 'Once when Jagjit was called to sing at Hridaynath's Ganpati Puja, I sat behind him on the platform. Everyone from the Mangeshkar family was there, including Meena, Usha and Lata. After a few songs, Jagjit said, "Hear one song from Chitra also," and asked me to take the mike. When I started singing, Lata got up and went away. Later, as we were leaving, I bent down to touch her feet, and she stepped back. I concluded that she did not like or approve of my singing.'

Perhaps he never mentioned it to Chitra then, but Jagjit nursed, along with his ambition of becoming a playback singer, the wish to sing with Lata someday. Of course, it was a fantastic dream. He had yet to get his own break.

Tumko dekha to ye khayal aaya
Zindagi dhoop tum ghana saaya

Aaj phir dil ne ek tamanna ki
Aaj phir dil ko hamne samajhaaya

Tum chale jaoge to sochenge
Humne kya khoya humne kya paaya

Hum jise gunguna nahi sakte
Waqt ne aisa geet kyun gaaya

A SHOULDER TO LEAN ON: CHITRA WITH JAGJIT

IN CONCERT

11

Jagjit Singh was a gentle soul. Never inclined to hurt by word or deed, he still had in him a core of steel that showed up when he took on the role of a teacher. Leading Chitra into his world of music, he trained her in diction, pitch and singing ability, till her voice rose and fell as he desired, and became a perfect complement to his own.

Recordings were always live. He would not brook even the idea of dubbing the voices over the music tracks. The recordings would be scheduled for one or two songs at a time. The musicians would also play live.

By 1970, Jagjit had found his own band of musicians who played the guitar, percussion, sitar, etc. The musicians would travel with him when, later, his tours began. Many would remain with him almost through their entire careers.

If there was any mistake during the recording, Jagjit would notice it immediately. He could catch a wrong note by a single instrument even in a multi-instrument ensemble. The recording would be stopped at once and the problem located and corrected.

With Chitra, he was a strict teacher. 'If I made a mistake while recording a duet, he would make a face. Or grunt, which would mean, "do it again". I would do it until he was satisfied. Yet, I felt, even from the very beginning, that he was indulgent with me. I often got the feeling that he would have preferred to go solo. He had almost said once that he had to compromise because of my singing with him. And he was right. While my voice was like a flute, thin and high-pitched, his had a strong bass to it. He was highly trained as a singer, I was completely untaught till he took me in hand.

'He could develop a song, embroider on it for long if he so desired. I could not do that. I could at most beautify what was given to me with a little change here and there. I could not improvize on a song of three minutes for forty-five minutes.

'I know it cramped his style, especially in the duets. More so on the stage. He could read the audience perfectly. When on his own, he would check audience response and take flights, expanding the raga, embellishing it. But he could not do that in the duets. Whereas, even in the duets he would have loved to fly away. It was his basic nature, to fly. He hated being restricted.

'Yet, I have heard him tell singers, who tried to copy my style, to listen to me carefully and correct themselves. He knew I could accomplish what he expected of me.'

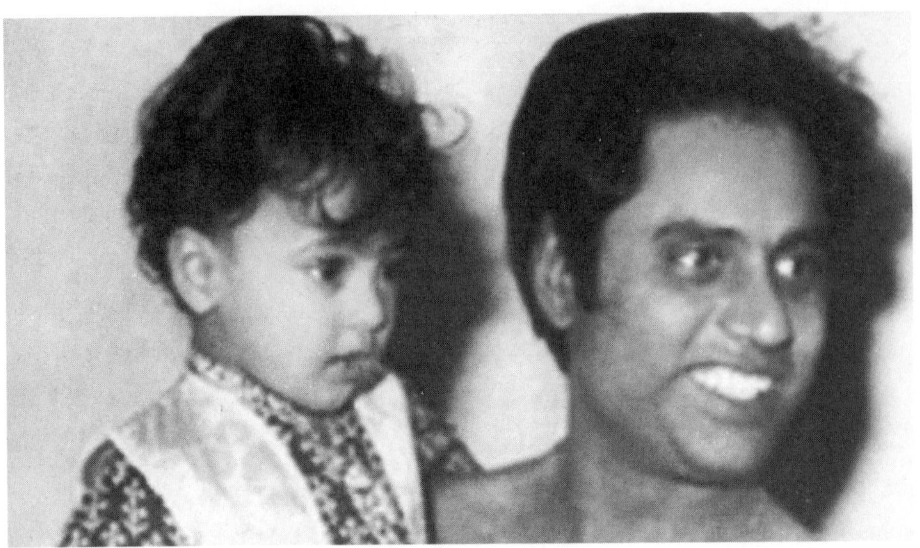

Jagjit with Baboo

Not surprisingly, Chitra too nourished the dream of singing playback. But it was never to be. 'I once sang in a live performance with Mukesh. I came into contact with Kishore Kumar who offered me an Africa tour, but for a very small amount of money. I met many music directors, people like Ravi. But most were uncomfortable with me because of my background and upbringing. Madan Mohan loved my voice and became a good friend, but he died before we could work together. Jaidev was another good friend. He wanted to use my voice, but film producers didn't want me. Roshan was another music director who liked my voice, and I was all set to sing for *Anokhi Raat*, but his wife requested me to back off, and that was the end of that.'

But Jagjit encouraged his wife, recording two EPs between 1969 and 1973, in which she sang both duets and solo. The duo also recorded a Super Seven record, a twenty-minute format that enjoyed brief popularity before it went out of the market. The songs included '*Jab bhi aati hai teri yaad*' and '*Dhuan uttha tha deewane ke*'.

Jagjit Singh also recorded two solo EPs. The records sold well. Despite the fact that the ghazal was not a popular form of song, with only a few directors favouring it, the public took to the records that Jagjit Singh put out in the market.

In 1971, a year after their wedding, their son Vivek was born. In true Bengali tradition, he was quickly given a nickname, Baboo. Jagjit and Chitra too adopted nicknames: henceforth they would call each other Papa and Mama. Money was still a problem. Chitra had to concentrate on the baby, and the house seemed smaller than ever. She kept busy with household chores and being a mother. But naturally, in the cramped space, the one who felt the pinch the most was Monica. However, the love showered on her by her mother and stepfather, and her fascination with the newborn only helped knit the family closer. Baboo was a beautiful baby, combining the good looks of both his parents. Little wonder that his parents doted on him beyond reason. For Jagjit, it seemed his world had suddenly blossomed. Chitra, despite the tribulations of managing home and baby all by herself, felt, 'joy, such joy'.

Jagjit remembers, 'In my life so far, I can say there have been three defining moments, turning points, call them whatever you like. The first was on 20 August 1971 when Baboo was born. I remember it was in the afternoon at 1.44 p.m. in Breach Candy Hospital. That was the height of happiness. We were not well off then, but I felt I was the richest man in the world.'

Work had to go on. The home fires had to keep burning. And a baby is always an expensive proposition. Chitra admits she was a fastidious and obsessive mother. When she had to record her first jingle after Baboo was born, she swaddled the twenty-day-old baby, carried him into the recording studio, and held him sleeping in her arms as she sang into the mike. In fact, after that she bravely took on more assignments, carrying her baby along without a second thought. It was a time which the Singhs remembered as among the happiest in their lives.

The fact that money was sporadic and sparse, that they lived in a cramped space where the room turned into living and sleeping space as per time and need, seemed of no import. If there is one regret that Chitra still has, it is that her daughter, cramped for space, had to move back into her father's house. She undoubtedly must have been much more comfortable there, with a room of her own and a better quality of living, but she must have missed the life she was used to as she shifted out. Chitra, preoccupied with the new baby, neglected understanding the feelings of a sensitive girl, who was on the verge

HAPPY TIMES: CHITRA WITH BABOO

In tune with each other

of turning into a teenager. And as the future would show, it would become cause for eternal regret.

Despite all this, the family stayed closely knit. Monica adored her little brother, and mothered him without reservation. The child, in turn, would turn his big blue eyes towards her in simple adoration. Monica was bright and talented, her mind quick to grasp things. Baboo's qualities would reveal themselves as the years went by. He would show a natural aptitude for playing the tabla by ear, even as a toddler. But all that lay hidden in the misty future. For now, he was treated to his parents' world of music, accompanying them whenever they went for performances at night, sleeping blissfully, fists curled near his baby head, on a tiny mattress spread out for him behind his parents at the back of the stage.

ON TOUR IN KARACHI AND ISLAMABAD, PAKISTAN

The 1970s were the golden age of Hindi film music. When the music left the cinema halls and reached into homes and hearts, it matured into something that did not need scene and story to support it and keep it alive. Just the singer, the words and the composition were enough to create a mood, convey an emotion and tell each listener a story that he felt was completely his own.

Jagjit Singh was approached by HMV to record an album by himself. This was no EP with only four songs but a full-fledged LP. Long playing records had come into the Indian market with a bang. They held all the songs of a film, often accommodating as many as ten to twelve compositions. Art departments in music companies thought it a happy challenge to design jackets for the larger format covers. Printing too had improved considerably and the music stores proudly stacked up colourful LPs that vied with one another for the music buff's attention. There was a sudden excitement in recording his first LP, and Jagjit communicated it to Chitra with the air of a boy talking about the marbles he had won against his rivals.

By now, Jagjit Singh was touring quite a bit. His stage shows were becoming popular. The shy, quiet and introvert singer had blossomed into a performer. He realized the power his music had over his listeners; he could seduce them, mesmerize them. It gave him the confidence to start engaging his listeners in musical conversations or narrating small stories and jokes.

Whether it was a concert in Bombay or in a small town like Nagpur, he realized that a joke was not only an ideal way to break the ice and give the audience a change of pace, but also a way to ensure his accompanists got a break. Jagjit fans have, over the years, created small compilations of his jokes, and shared them through word of mouth or on the Internet.

Two such bear repetition, though here they will lack the soft, earnest tone of voice that Jagjit used in his narratives.

The first joke was narrated at a show in Glasgow in 1993: 'There is a big store in Delhi, quite like the one owned by Salli sahab in Glasgow, but the Delhi store sold only liquor. One evening, when the owner was at home, after shutting the shop for the day, the telephone rang. Someone asked him, "Lala-ji, when does your shop open tomorrow?" The owner responded, "At 10 in the morning. It is closed for the day now." After an hour, the phone rang again. A much deeper voice asked him if it was Lala-ji speaking, and asked when the store would open. The owner responded that it would open at 10 a.m. The phone rang again after half an hour, and a voice, slurring as it spoke, asked him when his liquor store would open in the morning. Recognizing the caller, and realizing that he must be desperate, Lala-ji told him, "Does not matter, you come now, you seem desperate. I will give you what you want." "That is not the case," the man answered, "I am not desperate. You see I am asking because you have shut the shop and gone and I am still inside."'

Then there is the joke of the good-looking, fair-skinned young man who came to Bombay to seek his fortune. In Jagjit's words, 'After the first few days of going around and meeting people hoping for a break but getting none, he realized his money was almost finished. But he was hungry and had to buy some food. He decided to find something in the market that would be cheap but filling. His eyes caught sight of a watermelon, which proved real value for money. In Bombay, watermelons could be bought for five or six rupees, and he was sure he could fill his stomach with the fruit. He carried it to a spot under a tree, and settled down to eat. When he cut into the watermelon, smoke started coming out of it. Following the smoke a genie emerged. Laughing ho ho ha ha ha as genie are wont to doing, he addressed the man, "Master, what is your command?" Overjoyed at the fact that all his wishes would be fulfilled, the young man said, "I am hungry, get me food." Immediately the genie got food for his master from Balbir Singh's restaurant. Then the man asked for decent clothes, necessary to make a good impression when he set out again to meet influential people. A dozen suits were lined up for him in the blink of an eye. The man then said, "I need a place to live, find me one; even a small flat will do." But before he could complete his sentence, the genie stopped him. "Master," he said, and he spoke very seriously, "if I could find a flat in Bombay, would I live inside a watermelon?"'

It was a new method of entertainment, very different from the staid, structured, strait-jacketed ghazal singing that was the norm; and the audience loved it. The tours supplemented the meagre earnings from jingles and royalties. For the first time, Jagjit Singh could fulfil his filial duties and send money

On tour in Dubai

home to his parents. And to his utter relief, his father, who had severed ties with him when he cut his hair, had reconciled to the fact, spurred by the knowledge of his son's success. Though, secretly, the senior told himself that someday his son would grow his hair back and roll it under a turban once again!

'When he was not travelling, Jagjit would sit at home and compose.' Chitra recounts the lead up to the recording of *The Unforgettables*. 'One day he came back from a meeting with HMV and told me, "They want me to do an LP." I was a little hurt. "They asked only you?" I queried. "They know we are together, married, we have two EPs each. How come then ...?" He looked at me and said, "No. They said nothing about you."

'Then suddenly I realized I was also to sing for the LP.'

One can now only speculate whether *The Unforgettables* would have developed into a timeless creation and made the kind of musical history it did without Chitra. Jagjit included two of his most popular stage numbers, '*Baat niklegi*' and '*Ahista ahista*' in it, which should have made the LP a bestseller anyway. The other solos were equally beautiful, an ideal mix of lyrics and mood.

JAGJIT AND CHITRA WITH VIVEK AT CARNEGIE HALL

ON TOUR IN TORONTO

If *'Gham badhe aate hain qatil ki nigahon ki tarah'* has its place in the pantheon of unforgettable songs, so does the other Jagjit solo, *'Dost ban ban ke mile mujh ko mitane wale'*.

Many detractors of Chitra's voice, who found her no match for Jagjit Singh's polished control over his art, were quietened by the perfection of the new LP. Chitra's solos like *'Ek na ek shamma'*, and the duets *'Aaye hain samjhane log'* and *'Bahut pehle se'* provided a pleasing counterpoint, a foil to the masculinity of Jagjit's solos. Moreover the arrangement of the music, the use of non-traditional instruments, and the choice of lyrics added a charming wistfulness to the songs.

Once the LP was recorded, the duo set off on a tour, accompanied by the two children. Sheikh Abdul Razaq of Kuwait had sent an invitation, which they accepted. Then they visited Dubai, and finally, deciding on a much-needed holiday, the family went to London. A suitcase full of summer clothes had to be emptied out for the woollens they had to buy to tackle the London cold. Sometime in this period, news reached them that the LP had been released. There was no indication of how it had been received. It would be six months before the Singh family returned to realize that the LP was a hit! Already, it had earned for the normally cash-strapped Jagjit the impressive sum of 80,000 rupees.

The Unforgettables stormed the public consciousness like a new singer had, many years ago, by singing *'Aayega aanewala'*.

A musical revolution had begun, and even the duo who had launched it were surprised by its force.

Baat niklegi to phir door talak jaayegi,
Log be-wajah udaasi ka sabab poochhenge,
Yeh bhi poochhenge ki tum itni pareshaan kyun ho,
Ungliyaan uthengi sukhe huye baalon ki taraf,
Ik nazar dekhenge guzre huye saalon ki taraf,
Choodiyon par bhi kai tanz kiye jaayenge,
Kaanpte haathon pe bhi fikre kase jaayenge,
Log zaalim hain, har ik baat ka taana denge,
Baaton baaton mein mera zikr bhi ley aayenge,
Unki baaton ka zara sa bhi asar mat lena,
Varna chehre ke taasur se samajh jaayenge,
Chaahe kuchh bhi ho sawaalaat na karna unse,
Mere baare mein koi baat na karna unse,
Baat niklegi to phir door talak jaayegi

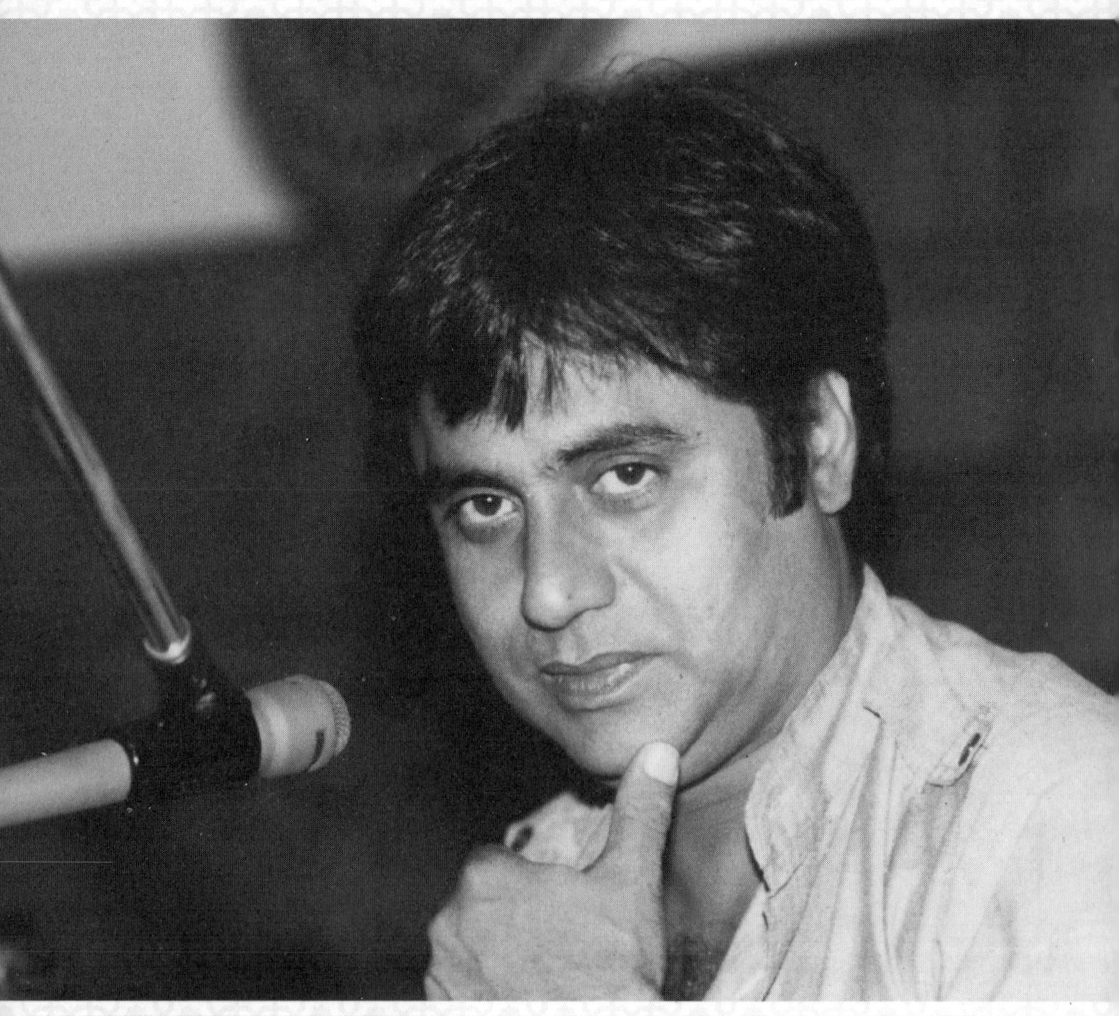

LOOKING THE AUDIENCE IN THE EYE

Though he had been singing ghazals, setting poems on offbeat themes to music by himself, almost at all his public performances, the risk involved in creating an LP of ghazals was considerable.

Looking at the popularity of the earlier EP recordings by Jagjit, Amit Sood of HMV took the chance.

As he started selecting the songs he would keep on the record, choosing from ghazals and nazms, Jagjit was also deciding on the form his music would take. He would compose the tunes and imagine the instruments that would support his voice. Whether it was because he wished to give the ghazal a younger, more contemporary appeal, or because he had himself been influenced by the guitars he had heard through his college days at musical competitions, the singer decided that the instrument would be part of the ensemble. The orchestration would remain simple, not more than four or five instruments. For Jagjit, the tune and music formed a setting for the words. Lyrics were paramount; through them he would reach the heart of the listener.

There is no explanation as to why a singer or composer adopts a particular form of composition as his favoured one. The ghazal had its patrons. The form was perfect for expressing pain and loss, or the sweet agonies of unrequited love. Poets from the 6th century had been writing verse with a decided form and a rhyming pattern and structure that was almost sacrosanct, even as the ghazal developed and evolved, moving from Arabic to Persian and then Urdu. In the12th century, Sufi mystics took up the form and added the passion for the Divine into its lines. The scope of the poem expanded to contain within its frame of rhyming couplets, lines that could be read at once as earthly or divine yearning. The beloved became a theme translatable by the listener according to his mood or leanings.

The ghazal, still an Islamic tradition, entered the Indian classical tradition at a time when records were not maintained about the singers or the songs they sang. The oral tradition, however passed on some of the poems as well as the music. But the ghazal remained, through the ages, a form that was appreciated by the very few, who were not just literate enough to understand the double-edged words in their complexity but also connoisseurs of music to the extent of appreciating the classical ragas the poems were set in.

Even when Begum Akhtar, breaking tradition, lent her powerful voice to the ghazal, shattering the walls of exclusivity that had held it confined, it was not imagined to be a popular genre of music.

If the ghazal did indeed get some measure of popularity, it was thanks to the film world. Singers like G.M. Durrani, Noor Jehan and Mohammed Rafi sang ghazals in films, and in private albums, which their popularity helped sell. Talat Mahmood, what with his tremulous lover's voice full of longing and suppressed passion, set the ghazal soaring to a new high. Singing easier-to-understand poems set to semi-classical or simple tunes made the ghazal a means of touching the heart of the lay listener. Composer Madan Mohan took the genre to a new level of popularity in films like *Aakhri Khat*, *Dastak*, *Anpadh* and later *Mausam*.

Film music directors experimented quite a bit with the ghazal, and the story of how S.D. Burman took '*Tadbeer se bigdi hui taqdeer bana le*', a ghazal written by Sahir Ludhianvi, for the film *Baazi* to a new place by setting it to a zany tune with a guitar as the main accompaniment, is now part of film music legend.

It was inevitable that Jagjit Singh would seize the chance of composing for his first LP to impress on the music world his stamp of originality. He already had some instrumentalists working regularly on tours with him. He decided they would share the unforgettable moments of the making of this LP.

Listen to the first three numbers on the LP, and the extent of Jagjit's experiment is already evident. In the first song, the guitar strums right from the start. First-time listeners in 1975 must have been surprised by the song that followed. Those who had heard it live at shows, of course, must have been thrilled to have it in their possession at last. Either way, the song, with its lyrics, singing and contemporary appeal, would continue to enjoy the popularity it first gained as a novelty.

Chitra's ghazal that follows the first number, on the other hand, uses other instruments: the sarangi and tabla, old companions of the ghazal form.

And in '*Ahista ahista*', another perennial number, the beat spelt out by what sounds like the shekere, an African hand-held instrument, is almost a precursor of what another music wizard R.D. Burman would do, in combining Eastern and Western classical and folk musical instruments in his compositions.

While the lay public and even the knowledgeable among music aficionados reached out to embrace the offering, purists were, and expectedly so, offended. Jagjit took it in his stride. 'I have been criticized for the use of instrumentation and ghazal composition. People say, "This is hardly a ghazal! Ghazal is not(sung) like this!" To which I reply, "*Aap bataiye kaisi hoti hai?*"

'If you say Begum Akhtar's was the only style of ghazal, I can't accept that. Her style reflects her milieu: that doesn't mean it is a formula for others to follow. Before her, Barkat Ali had his own style. *This* is my style. What is to be seen now is who is better accepted. Whichever is widely accepted becomes in the long run the tradition. Different styles can flourish side by side.'

Shantanu Ray Chaudhuri, Managing Editor at HarperCollins Publishers India and a keen Jagjit follower, presents the case for Jagjit's popularity, 'He made the ghazal sound cool with Western instruments and stereophonic recording. I came under the spell of ghazals in my twenties, primarily because I liked the sound of the beats when compared to much better renditions by stalwarts like Begum Akhtar and Mehdi Hassan

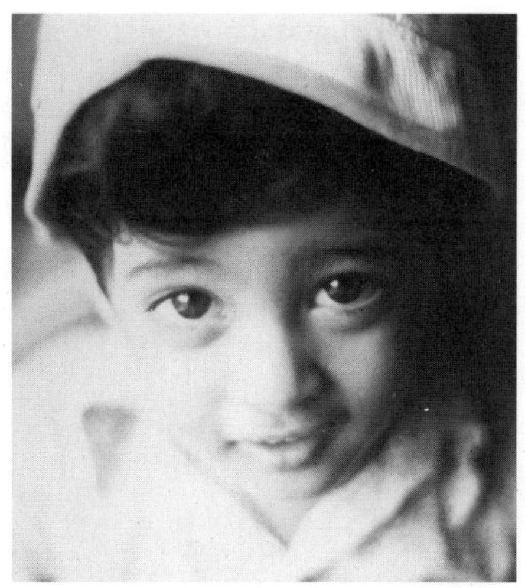

Vivek as a boy

(which took time for me to develop an understanding of), who were more traditional. It was Jagjit who got me keen on the ghazal.'

The Unforgettables set the style. In it, Jagjit Singh combines the traditional sarangi and tabla with the sitar, the guitar, the saxophone, piano, and the double bass. One of the inspirations for this, he admitted, was Khayyam. But of course, he took the inspiration and made the style entirely his own.

Poets and writers, however, joined the listener in speaking for *The Unforgettables* and all it stood for. 'The soul of the ghazal is the metre, which you can't tamper with, which Jagjit has never done. The language of poetry is never simple, it is not the language of the tea stall

The singer and the composer

LISTEN TO THE FIRST THREE NUMBERS ON THE LP, AND THE EXTENT OF JAGJIT'S EXPERIMENT IS ALREADY EVIDENT. IN THE FIRST SONG, THE GUITAR STRUMS RIGHT FROM THE START. FIRST-TIME LISTENERS IN 1975 MUST HAVE BEEN SURPRISED BY THE SONG THAT FOLLOWED. THOSE WHO HAD HEARD IT LIVE AT SHOWS, OF COURSE, MUST HAVE BEEN THRILLED TO HAVE IT IN THEIR POSSESSION AT LAST. EITHER WAY, THE SONG, WITH ITS LYRICS, SINGING AND CONTEMPORARY APPEAL, WOULD CONTINUE TO ENJOY THE POPULARITY IT FIRST GAINED AS A NOVELTY.

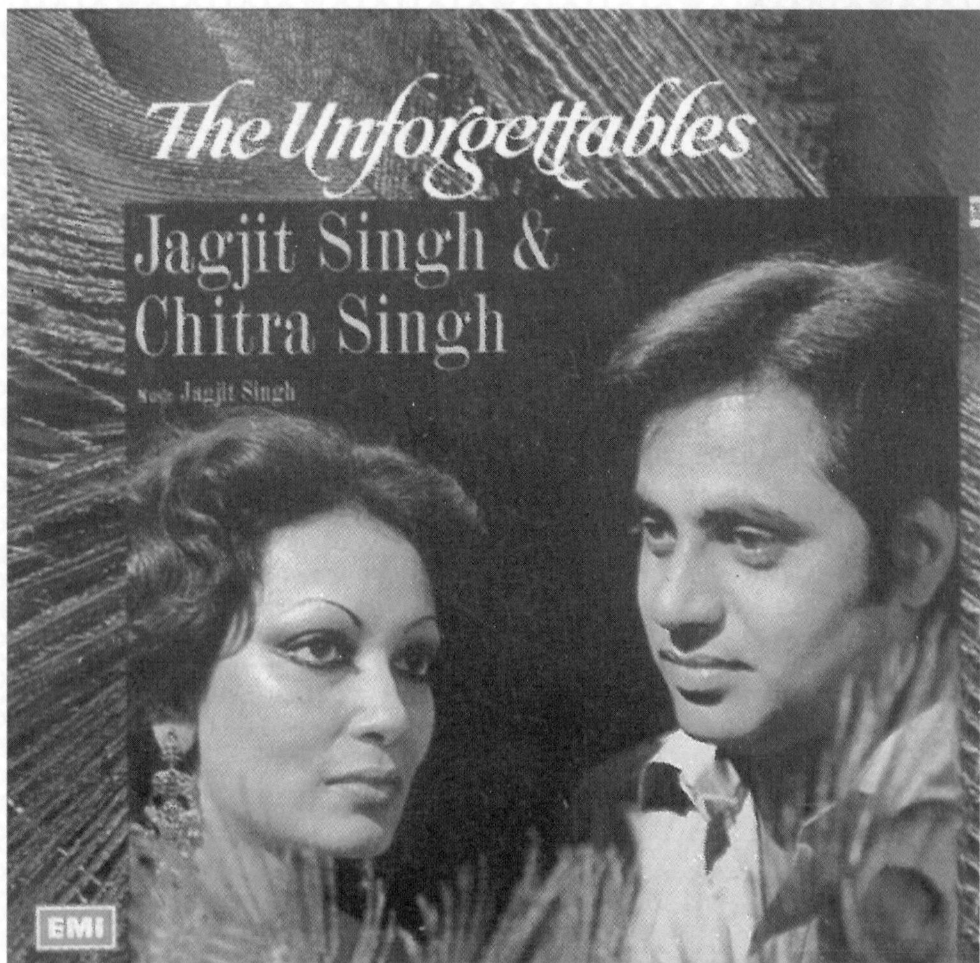

THE COVER OF THEIR FIRST LP

after all, but he made the singing style so attractive that people wanted to understand even the most difficult words of the poem. When the Urdu language was on the decline, he rekindled interest in the language and its poetry and gifted the tongue with a new life. That's a big contribution,' Rana Sahri, the poet, says.*

Jagjit himself has shared stories about *The Unforgettables* that still hold meaning. One of them is about *'Baat niklegi'*. Realizing its popularity with his listeners at shows, Jagjit sent it to HMV, which was producing an album with his friend Bhupinder singing Jagjit's compositions. After the first recording of the first number, which happened to be this one, Jagjit asked for a couple of retakes, feeling that the rendition could be improved. Sensitive as most artistes are, Bhupinder took the request to be a censure of his singing and backed out of the project.

The song was then recorded in Jagjit's own voice for a film that never saw the light of day. And so *'Baat niklegi'* was finally included in *The Unforgettables* as its opening nazm.

Keeping the trend of creating attractive LP covers in mind, *The Unforgettables* too would be bright, colourful and yet showcase the sophistication of the music it packaged. 'My ex-husband, Dutta, Jagjit and I designed the cover,' Chitra said, 'but the title was given by my father. Prophetic, was it not?'

**The quote has been taken from the book* Beyond Time, *a limited edition published by Pankaj Kodesia & Associates in 2002*

A HAPPY THREESOME: JAGJIT, CHITRA AND VIVEK

Chitra's parents were in Calcutta still, when she married Jagjit Singh. 'They did not keep very good health. So, when Baboo was born in 1971, we took him to his grandparents. I also had to introduce Jagjit to them; they had not met him either,' says Chitra Singh. In fact, the parents were not even aware that Chitra had undergone a divorce, let alone remarried. Chitra had written to her mama, and the uncle had advised her to visit her parents when they came for the performance scheduled at the Kalamandir on Theatre Sarani in Calcutta.

Surprisingly, by the time they were due to return to Bombay, it was decided that her parents would shift out of Calcutta. 'Everybody in my family felt it was part of my responsibility, and when Jagjit got wind of this, in his characteristic way, he said they must stay with us.'

By 1975, the singers were in a position to put the plan to action. 'We took a loan and bought a low-priced I-BHK in Bandra for them.' Despite this, Chitra felt guilty. She was in Warden Road while her parents were in Bandra, and in poor health, unable to look after themselves properly.

There are countless stories of Jagjit Singh's ability to reach out and help others in need, but Chitra avows that he 'bought me(her) over for twelve lifetimes' by being a son to her parents. He was always there whenever they needed someone, and her father would proudly say that Jagjit was his son.

True to his word and intention, Jagjit ensured that his parents-in-law moved in with him and Chitra a year after they shifted to Bombay.

As luck would have it, a flat in the building the singers lived in fell vacant. A lot of negotiations and some sticky situations later, the Singh family—Chitra, Jagjit and the child—moved into a house on the ground floor of the same building. They had to pay almost three times the original price for the space. The Bandra flat that Chitra's parents had vacated lay unoccupied as it found no buyers. Five years later, it would be occupied by Monica, who by then had become a top model and married cameraman Jehangir Chowdhury.

Jagjit and Chitra also dutifully visited Ludhiana to let Jagjit's family meet its new entrant. 'Jagjit's father was deeply religious and there were many rites and ceremonies around the one-year-old Baboo, as there were on a host of other occasions too,' Chitra recollects. It was a big house, peopled with the family, and she remembers, how at 5 a.m., her

CHITRA'S DAUGHTER MONICA

A LEADING MODEL OF HER TIME

father-in-law would clatter about the U-shaped *aangan* in his wooden *khadaaus*, while he recited from the Guru Granth Sahib.

'Jagjit's sisters took me with a pinch of salt. I was too different. They had heard that their brother had married a divorcee with a child and thought she must have "*phasaaoed*" him. On the other hand, they were in awe of me, and as I gave them no reason to dislike me, they had to eventually accept me.' Chitra still displays a quiet smoldering anger over the fact that in a rather cavalier manner, Jagjit did not prepare her for the visit and the meetings. Despite knowing that his father was cut up with him, he had taken her there, and she wondered why.

When the family came to know that Jagjit was setting up a home, 'everybody came to pay a visit. Elder brother, wife, son, daughter, their children, his married sister and her two sons, as well as the sister from Rajasthan—everyone came.' Chitra still rankles a bit at their judgmental ways. 'Baboo was still on the bottle, I used to sterilize the rubber. They thought it was a lot of fuss. We were different.'

Suddenly, Chitra was exposed to a part of her husband's life that she had not known existed. Once the family left, the friends came along. This sometimes led to disagreements between the couple.

'The women of the household were completely taken for granted,

Social evenings

relegated to the kitchen and to caring for others. When in Ludhiana, I noticed that his mother would get up at 4 a.m. and enter the kitchen and start working. She would serve hot food whenever anyone came in. And people would drop in all the time. There would be *manjis* in the courtyard; they would sit there and eat. My father-in-law would invite all visitors to a meal without any consultation with his wife. Often, the last bit of food would be fed to an unexpected guest. My father-in-law would come across as magnanimous, but my mother-in-law would sometimes have to go hungry. No one cared.

'When in his turn, Jagjit did the same thing, asking his friends who dropped in, to stay for dinner, I used to get angry. "At least ask me first," I would say. "You cannot be generous at someone else's cost."'

In fact, there were many little adjustments that the Singhs found marriage urged them into. Mostly, they were from Chitra's side. 'When Baboo was five months old, a musician visited us, and wanted to see him. I brought him out and the man kissed him. When I protested, he said, "I have had a bath today, so why should I not kiss the child?" Jagjit too reprimanded me, saying I was too *angrez*.'

Kartar, Jagjit's younger brother, came to stay. 'We were on the seventh floor when he came to visit. When we moved down to the ground floor, he was still there, except for some visits out of Bombay.' Kartar Singh, the youngest, adored his brother. He also made himself useful, driving his nephew to school. The car which Chitra's ex-husband had given them was still there, but he had discontinued the driver once the Singhs married.

'I finished my graduation and went to stay with my brother,' Kartar recollects. 'That was in 1978-'79. I was there for three years, then came back to look after my parents.'

Kartar has pleasant memories of the period. Jagjit was busy with films, and a bevy of music directors and writers like Sudarshan Faakir and Saeed Rahi were in and out of the house. Besides this, like-minded singers who were also fond of singing ghazals would visit all the time. Ashok Khosla, Abhijeet, Hariharan, Vinod Saigal... There would be rehearsals and music through the day. 'It was one of his most productive periods, '*Kaaghaz ki kashti*', '*Tum itna jo*', were all created, composed and sung during this phase.

'At first, I just sat and listened as I had done as a child, listening

Celebrating Baboo's birthday with Monica

'JAGJIT'S FATHER WAS DEEPLY RELIGIOUS AND THERE WERE MANY RITES AND CEREMONIES AROUND THE ONE-YEAR-OLD BABOO, AS THERE WERE ON A HOST OF OTHER OCCASIONS TOO,' CHITRA RECOLLECTS. IT WAS A BIG HOUSE, PEOPLED WITH THE FAMILY.'

AT AN HMV DISC PRESENTATION

Left to right: Mr Abbas, Recording Executive; V.K. Dubey, VP HMV; and Sanjeev Kohli, GM Artistes and Repertoire

JOHNNY BAKSHI(L) AND FRIEND(R) WITH JAGJIT

to his riyaz,' Kartar remembers. 'But later, Bhaisaab started coaxing me to learn singing. He said, "Do riyaz," and bought me a tanpura, which he tuned to match my voice, and made me sing. I sang once or twice.' Whenever Jagjit would, in later years too, visit Kartar in Delhi, the matter of his singing would come up. 'Once when I told him the tanpura was out of tune and that was why I had given up singing, he said, "I will find a solution to that," and got me an electronic tanpura!'

Kartar's stay with his elder brother opened up a new page in the closeness of the siblings. Even when the family went on their first visit to America, Kartar went along. Monica too was happy to have someone closer to her age around. She would take him along and introduce him to her friends. Chitra pushed Kartar to study, do his M.A. Jagjit would mockingly say, '*Aay may english karo.*'

But he took it upon himself to provide for everybody once he started earning well. When his father retired from looking after his business, Jagjit bought a house in Ghaziabad for his parents, and told them to sell the old place, which was unwieldy to maintain. Kartar was married in Ghaziabad, and his son was born a year later. Later, Jagjit wanted everyone to shift to Delhi, but his father passed away before the shift could take place.

Unlike his mother, Baboo was able to assimilate with his father's family wonderfully. Chitra remembers that he liked visiting Ghaziabad, and while there turned totally vegetarian and took to roaming around on a motorcycle. 'We worried about his missing fish and meat, but he was happy and actually said the food there was the highlight of his trips.'

And later, when he visited Kartar Singh in Delhi, when he was around ten or eleven, Baboo thoroughly enjoyed his uncle's company and wanted to stay with him as long as he could.

Jagjit's star was rising through this time. The popularity of *The Unforgettables* resulted in shows not only in far-off places like Patna and Agra, but many overseas requests came pouring in too. Wherever people heard the record, they wanted to see the artistes, hear them live. The image the songs and the LP jacket invoked was of a fresh, urbane couple, who dressed in contemporary fashion, seemed well educated and yet sang in a divinely entertaining manner.

Adding to the thrust of their songs was the fact that film music was starting on a decline. The

Conversing in ghazals: Jagjit with Javed Akhtar

wonderful music of the 1960s and early '70s had already begun to blend into the styles that would rule in the '80s. While a new generation of filmgoers took to the new songs, those who had grown up on melody were left bereft. Of the thirty or so films released in 1975, only ten or so had music that resonated with listeners. Among them *Chupke Chupke*, *Mili*, (both from a fading S.D. Burman) *Mausam*, *Aandhi* (which had Gulzar, Madan Mohan and R.D. Burman ensuring good lyrics and tunes), *Sholay*, which succeeded thanks to the film's success rather than the quality of its music, and themes for young, frothy films like *Hero*, and *Khel Khel Mein*, which had foot-tapping numbers to suit hero Rishi Kapoor's nimble footwork. Of course, there was also the thundering success of *Jai Santoshi Maa*, which appealed to a different set of audiences or listeners.

Little wonder then that the 'Singh-ing' duo were invited to the most prestigious performance venues. Chitra lists them: Carnegie Hall, Royal Albert Hall... nothing was left to be explored. The audience was mostly Indian of course, but whether it was in the US, Australia, the Gulf or England, almost 20 per cent of the audience comprised local populace. Their music transcended the barriers of language.

It is almost a well-known fact that Jagjit never did riyaz. 'He would never rehearse during tours; to him, his show was his rehearsal. Sometimes he would not even decide on the songs. He would size up the audience within minutes of going onstage, and decide how to woo them with his music.' He had an impressive memory. Chitra recollects that he would remember the words of every single song. The books would be there, even opened to the correct page by helpful hands on stage, but he would not even glance at them. Chitra, on the other hand, needed to keep them handy. In fact, so high was Jagjit's confidence in his songs, that once, much later, while touring South Africa, when his luggage did not arrive with him, Jagjit borrowed a kurta from someone and went on to start his programme. Abhinav, his tabla player, and Deepak Pandit would prompt him onstage should he falter at a word or forget a line. But it was a show that brought the house down anyway. Chitra also knew exactly how to keep in step. Coordination was a series of signals that their proximity as a couple helped her understand perfectly. After each song, Jagjit would turn the pages of their notebook to the next song to let Chitra know, and he would share a look when he wished to take flight with a tune at any particular moment, and wanted Chitra to stay silent.

Such was the popularity of the Singhs that when AIR and the press boycotted them in later years, after their visit to South Africa, since India was anti-apartheid, the couple continued to hold their own without the publicity.

All through the months and years after *The Unforgettables*, Jagjit kept composing. Chitra would be around doing her chores—bathing the child, cooking, sometimes even doing the dishes. Once the tune was finalized, it would be obvious—she could make it out. But rehearsals would take place for the first time only at the recording studio.

Chitra's memory of how he composed his tunes is vivid still. 'When he got a poem, he would immediately check its metre and find a taal to match. Then he would explore till he found a tune to match the taal. He would go easy, not forcing it at all. He would scan the song, trying to see where to break a line, where to take a breath, without changing its meaning. The tune, of course, would be happy, or soft, or sad, in keeping with the mood of the lyrics.'

LITTLE BABOO

LIFE WAS A GHAZAL

15

Even as their careers soared, the Singhs found great joy in their son. He was special. A darling boy, who was not just beautiful and obedient, but also seemed to be gifted with his parents' talent for music. Perhaps the fact that he had slept in his mother's arms as a twenty-day-old and backstage all through his infancy while his parents went from one show to the other, singing for hours on end, added to the natural gift.

Even before Chitra returned home from Breach Candy Hospital, six days after Baboo was born, Jagjit had appointed a servant exclusively to help her. 'He was a good man, from Orissa, and could lift Baboo when, at four months, he grew to be a big baby who looked six or seven months old.' Chitra devoted herself completely to her son. 'He and Benjamin Spock were my life. I took care of him by the letter. And as if he had read the book too, Baboo cried all night, most nights!

'Jagjit would be out, but on his return, he would immediately go to his son and pick him up. I would have walked him up and down, while he howled, but the moment his father held him, Baboo would quieten completely.'

Jagjit did offbeat things for his son. He would cut out lengths of mull and, layering them, stitch nappies for Baboo at night on Chitra's sewing machine, while the boy slept peacefully as if knowing his father was near. He would bathe the child, or give him oil massages. 'His touch was magical for the child, there was some special bond between them that I could not fathom.'

As Baboo grew up, Jagjit tried to spend as much time as he could with him, even though he was busy recording a series of albums and performing at shows. He was good at math and would teach the boy, while Chitra had the task of taking his English lessons. Until he turned six, they would take him to shows where he slept backstage through the performance. By the age of eight, he was playing the dholki on stage, starting with a show at Bombay's Bhaidas Hall; the audience loved the trio!

'Father and son were friends, he was not one bit scared of his father as so many children are,' Chitra underlines. She enrolled Baboo in the Sophia Nursery. Then he moved to Miniland in Pheroza Godrej's Cymroza Art Gallery. Jagjit would pick him up every day from there and take him to play cricket.

Even as a baby, when he could hardly reach the tabla top, Baboo would try to place his tiny hands

In august company: with the President of India, Shankar Dayal Sharma, and Mr and Mrs B.R. Chopra

'AT THAT TIME, SHANKAR DAYAL SHARMA WAS THE HIGH COMMISSIONER FROM INDIA. HE INVITED US HOME FOR A PRIVATE CONCERT. AS DID MANY INFLUENTIAL LOCAL BUSINESSMEN. WE CONTINUED TO GET INVITATIONS EVERY DAY, AND ONLY WHEN WE SHOWED THE NOTICE WE WERE GIVEN BY THE PAKISTAN GOVERNMENT TO LEAVE BY 20 FEBRUARY, WERE WE ALLOWED TO LEAVE.'

on it and play. Jagjit recognized his interest and appointed a tabla master to teach him the basics. Chitra believes that was a mistake. 'The regimentation drove him off, he just stopped playing the tabla. Later, he switched to drums.'

Even though the work increased and he got busy with programmes and films, Jagjit ensured he dropped and picked up his son when the boy moved to St. Mary's School in Byculla. Chitra was grateful to be spared the extra job, her hands were full, too, looking after her parents.

'Baboo was four-and-a-half when we went to Dubai,' remembers Chitra. The family then went to the UK where Baboo celebrated his fifth birthday. 'Mini(Monica) was also with us, but she had a modelling assignment and returned from the UK, while we went on to East Africa.'

They were halcyon days, when the family practically lived out of suitcases, and the music and travelling and shows never stopped. Celebrities now, they rubbed shoulders with royalty and showmen. Chitra remembers that Baboo cut his milk tooth in Trinidad, where they met Gaj Singh of Jodhpur, who was posted there as High Commissioner of India. 'He was a fan of Papa, and remains one to this day.'

Then the pace slackened, but only by choice. 'Once Baboo started school, we accepted tours only during his summer or Diwali vacations so he could accompany us. I think at most he may have missed coming along once or twice.'

One of the countries they did not take their son to was Pakistan. They went in 1979. The country seemed won over by the fact that Jagjit and Chitra were visiting. The newspapers had an entire page on the couple, the only other news on the front page was of Bhutto's impending hanging.

With Baboo in Dubai

'The political situation when we went was not very calm; we could sense a tension. When we landed, we noticed a man getting into the aircraft and just standing there. We saw him again and again. He followed us out of the airport, and we saw him again in the hotel. It was unnerving. The room bell rang, Jagjit opened the door, and he was outside. He entered. Jagjit asked him in Punjabi, "Are you following us?" He motioned to say the room was bugged, then explained that he was from the Intelligence Department. He was our fan. *Chori chori*, with utmost care, he drew out from inside his jacket a bottle wrapped in newspaper; he had brought alcohol as a gift since the hotel served none.

'Pakistan banned us from giving public performances. But the Press Club invited us privately, and we sang to a full house. There was a restless murmur about our presence in the newspapers. At that time, Shankar Dayal Sharma was the High Commissioner from India. He invited us home for a private concert, as did many influential local businessmen. We continued to get invitations every day, and only when we showed the notice we were given by the Pakistan government to leave by 20 February, were we allowed to leave. Otherwise, we might have had endless invitations from the large community of fans, who defied the government to listen to us.'

Later, much after 1990, Jagjit visited Pakistan alone. He met President Musharraf at his residence and the President played the tabla with him. And Kartar remembers Jagjit telling him how, when flying back from Islamabad to Delhi, the crew, knowing he was on board the flight, kept the aircraft in the air for two-and-a-half hours only to be longer in his company.

Many years later, Jagjit would prove how his music erased borders. When he took Baboo to the hotel where the Pakistan cricket team was staying during a tour in the early 1980s, so he could get all their autographs, the entire team took turns touching the singer's feet and saying, 'There is no one who sings like you do.' 'He had the knack of making every single person think he was singing only for him,' Kartar says.

Pakistan, Bangladesh, multiple trips to the US—the calendar was full of concerts. And the albums too kept coming. Jagjit and Chitra found time for it all.

Ghamaan di raat lammi eh
Ja mere geet lamme ne
Na bhedi raat mukdi eh
Na mere geet mukde ne

E sar kihne ku Doonge ne
Kise ne hath na paayi
Na barsaataan 'ch charde ne
Te na auraan 'ch sukhde ne

Mere had hi avahle ne
Jo ahg laaiyaan nahi sarde
Ne sarde haukeyaan de naal
Haavaan naal dhukde ne

ARRANGING MUSIC WITH ACE RECORDIST DAMAN SOOD

CELEBRATING THE SUCCESS OF *A SOUND AFFAIR*
V.K. Dubey of HMV, Peter Brown (then MD), Sanjeev Kohli with the singers

A staggering eighty albums owe their existence to Jagjit Singh. He sang in many languages, including Nepali. The LP that followed *The Unforgettables* was *Birha Da Sultan.*

Jagjit first met the poet Shiv Kumar Batalvi when he went to Simla as a student during the summer holidays. The popular Punjabi poet was being treated for TB over there. Both had time on their hands, and Batalvi was happy to have a gifted youngster wanting to meet him often. They would sit late into the night, reciting poetry, or the poet would hold mehfils, where perhaps young Jagjit would also participate by singing.

A year after *The Unforgettables*, by which time Batalvi had passed away, Jagjit approached HMV with the idea of bringing out a collection in the poet's memory. It would contain solos and duets to copy the format of *The Unforgettables.*

Jagjit selected some of the poet's best known ghazals, lacing the album with the mood of sadness that the poet evoked through his work. He took a leaf from the mehfils he had shared with Batalvi, where the poet used to recite his poems to a tune, and created his own music to recreate the original as closely as possible.

Birha Da Sultan, as the album was named, had an evocative jacket painted by none other than the artist Imroz, who was the poet—writer Amrita Pritam's partner till her death. In fact, it was Amrita Pritam who had first named Batalvi *'Birha Da Sultan'*, the Sultan of Sadness, due to the tone and tenor of his poetry.

The songs that Jagjit chose for the album included *'Ghamaan di raat lammi'*, *'Umraan de sarwar'*, *'Maye ni maye mere geetan de nainan vich'*, *'Rog banke reh gaya'*, *'Eh mera geet kise na gaana'*, *'Tusin kehri rutte aayel'*, *'Raat gayee kar tara tara'*, *'Jaach mainu aa gayee gham khaan di'*, *'Yaariyan rab karke'* and *'Maye ni main ik shikra yaar banaya'*, which he sang along with Chitra, in a style that had now become their hallmark.

Expectedly, the album was a huge hit in Punjab, where the poet is still

LP jacket of Birha Da Sultan

revered and where Jagjit has found a special place as its son.

It was around this time that a young man would enter Jagjit Singh's life. Together they would take up a thread that had unravelled many years ago, and with it, spin out an entire tapestry of dreams for Jagjit's fans.

Sanjeev Kohli did not associate Jagjit Singh with the songs he heard being played in the music room of the studio he worked with in Calcutta. He had possibly forgotten the drenched stranger he had accompanied with his parents to a mehfil in the house of Usha Raje. The music room was for listeners to preview their purchases. More than any other song, he caught the sound of mellifluous ghazals wafting out; the music seemed to have a haunting quality and weave itself around his mind.

At riyaz

After completing his MBA, still at an age when most graduates were looking for a job, Kohli had been absorbed by Polydor. The music company was just emerging as a player in the marketplace, and the idea was that the son of a music director would be able to bring in singers and other artistes more easily than others with the same educational qualifications.

As it happened, Kohli was chasing Mohammed Rafi. Rafi's contract with HMV was reportedly coming to an end, and Polydor was hoping to snap him up. Jagjit and Lata were out of reach, but Rafi would be a plum catch. Also, 'As I was Madan Mohan's son, and he had been the ghazal king, I had to do something to cash in on the growing popularity of the ghazal. If I could not get Jagjit, I had to find an alternative. It was a big decision, but I took it. I set out to discover new talent that was still waiting in the wings.' Kohli managed an impressive line-up: Penaz Masani, Talat Aziz, Anup Jalota and Pankaj Udhas. Polydor launched a host of new artistes in the ghazal genre.

There was no dearth of excitement. Rumour had it that

Rafi had had meetings with Jagjit, and there was some talk of a record in the offing. On instruction, Kohli met Rafi's brother-in-law to discuss the possibility of a non-film record. But there was no enthusiasm for the idea; the brother-in-law said he did not see how it could work.

Though he could not sing for Polydor, Jagjit Singh was persuaded to compose for them. As Rafi would not sing for them, Kohli decided to launch a new voice with Jagjit's compositions. He hit on the marketing plan of naming the record *Jagjit Singh Presents Talat Aziz*. No one knows how the songs would have sounded in Rafi's voice, but the new singer, with a name that recalled another ghazal maestro with an equally velvet voice and manners, managed to appeal to the public. Jagjit's name and music added to its weight. The album was a success.

The first step had been taken. A link had been forged between Polydor and Jagjit. It would lead Kohli and Jagjit to do their best work together.

The story of how Talat Aziz came to star in the album with Jagjit's compositions bears telling. Chitra remembers it clearly.

Jagjit and she were at a function in Hyderabad, which Talat and his parents attended. The next day they dropped by the hotel in which the Singhs were staying to invite them home to lunch. Chitra remembers the home as well laid out. The room they were welcomed into was lined with gaddas, and a mike stood ready for use. As the lunch progressed, she noticed that Talat Aziz wasn't eating. 'He will sing for you first, after that he will eat,' the boy's mother explained.

LP Jacket of Jagjit Singh Presents Talat Aziz

Jagjit and Chitra dutifully listened to the boy, who sang four or five songs, much in the Mehdi Hassan style. 'We made appropriate noises about his singing when he was done, and returned,' Chitra remembers.

A year later, Talat appeared at their door, a big smile on his face, hands folded in entreaty. He wanted to make a record, and requested Jagjit to introduce him to the industry. And of course, Jagjit, 'who was ever ready to help anyone who was struggling, like he himself had done', went a few steps ahead,' and the album was born.

'However, Papa was disappointed in the rendition of the songs, because he realized Talat Aziz had his limitations. Aziz treated them as songs to be sung, not internalized and rendered from the soul. But he rehearsed and recorded him all the same,' says Chitra.

Once it was known that Jagjit supported aspiring artistes, they flocked to him in droves. Chandan Das, who sang in a gentle manner that pleased Jagjit immensely; Anup Jalota, who moved away from his father's bhajans to climb on to the ghazal bandwagon; Pankaj Udhas; and Rajkumar Rizvi who even stayed for a few months at the Singh residence, because he had no means of his own. Everyone, in some way or the other, got a helping hand from Jagjit Singh and Sanjeev Kohli.

The new artistes Kohli brought to the fore fuelled the ghazal wave. The Singhs had paved the way; others followed in their wake. Soon, there would be other couples singing together. Rajendra and Nina Mehta, Bhupinder and Mitali, Roop Kumar Rathod and Sunalee—all of them built their own fan base. As did Anup Jalota, Talat Aziz, Pankaj Udhas, his brother Manhar and Penaz Masani.

At the release of the Bhajan *LP*

It was around then that Jagjit and Chitra's next album *Live at Wembley* hit the stores overseas. 'Our first proper tour of England was organized in 1979 by Pran Gohil, who was an associate of and dealer for Polydor,' Jagjit has recounted in the book *Beyond Time*. Gohil, confident of a total sell-out, had booked the Wembley Conference Centre for two nights over a weekend. He was able to cash in on the opportunity and organize a few more shows later on. Making the most of the tour, he also had a mobile studio record the concert. The live album was released in the UK, as Gohil had the foreign rights, and it was a big hit.

Kohli adds that the next album in the same year, titled *Come Alive*, released by HMV as a double, was recorded in the studios in Bombay, where the audience responses and applause were faked to make it seem live. It too was a runaway success. According to him, 'Jagjit repeated "*Ahista ahista*" in *Come Alive*, adding two new verses to complete the original poem by Ameer Minai:

Sarakati jaaye hai rukh se naqaab ahista ahista

Nikalta aa rahaa hai aftaab ahista ahista

Jawaan hone lage jab woh to ham se kar liya parda

Hayaa yakalakht aayi aur shabaab ahista ahista

Shab-e-furkat ka jaagaa hoon farishton ab to sone do

Kabhi fursat men kar lena hisaab ahista ahista

Savaal-e-vasl par unko uduu kaa khauf hai itna

Woh honthon se dete hain jawaab ahista ahista

Hamare aur tumhare pyaar mein bas farq hai itna

Idhar to jaldi jaldi hai udhar ahista ahista

Woh bedardi se sar kaate 'Ameer' aur main kahoon un se

Huzoor ahistaa ahistaa, janaab ahista ahista

The 'audience' responded as if they would like him to go on forever.

The tours and concerts were running parallel. Chitra said that in 1997, they performed at a record number of concerts: forty-two in the space of two-and-a-half months. Many years later, at the age of seventy, Jagjit would try to beat this record.

FILM POSTER OF *ARTH*

Then the time came when the tide started flowing backwards. It took Jagjit Singh towards realizing a very old dream, one he had almost forgotten about in the light of success.

Mahesh Bhatt was making his next film. Prone to mining for themes from his own life, this film was to explore and reveal the director's complex affair with actress Parveen Babi. Starring Shabana Azmi as the wife and Smita Patil as the mistress, it was to be called *Arth.* Kulbhushan Kharbanda would play the film director in it.

While most of the songs were to be penned by Kaifi Azmi, Bhatt turned to Jagjit for the music. The duo would also sing the songs. Jagjit had four songs, Chitra one. Finally, Chitra's dream was also coming true.

It was a movie crafted with raw passion and a lot of emotion. Mahesh Bhatt had real-life examples to lean on and he threw caution to the wind as he laid the dissolution of a marriage bare on screen.

The songs were sung onscreen by Raj Kiran, who would first empathize, then fall in love with the distraught, shattered wife of the filmmaker played by Kharbanda. They demanded music that was evocative and would pull at the viewer's heartstrings even as they drew out the heroine from despair towards self-reliance.

At a function after Jagjit Singh's death, to mark his birthday on 8 February, Shabana Azmi attributed some of her success in the role, which fetched her the National Film Award and also the Filmfare Award for Best Actress, to the music of the film, adding, 'I'm very fortunate that three of his most famous and popular songs were filmed on me in Mahesh Bhatt's *Arth.* The manner in which he so beautifully strung the lyrics with the pain that he was trying to convey left me with very little to do.'

By the time *Arth* happened in 1982, Jagjit had sung for a few other films. In Shatrughan Sinha's 1981 home production, *Prem Geet,* he had deliverd the solo, '*Hothon se chhoo lo tum*'.

Recordist Daman Sood remembers an incident about the song. 'The song was written by Indeevar, and it was being recorded live at the studio. Kuldeep Singh was arranging the music. Bhupinder was playing the guitar. I was also recording at Western Outdoor at the same time. It was a multi-track recording and one or two takes had just been completed. I could not help responding to the song, and told Indeevar, "What amazing lyrics, this song is sure to be a super hit." Indeevar smiled and said, "*Tumhare munh mein ghee shakkar.*" After three or four days, Jagjit said he wanted to re-record the song. He believed he had not given his best to it. I told him that was not possible. He tried anyway, singing different versions for the next few days. I held my peace, saying nothing. Finally, he agreed that the first version was the best. I realized later, he was trying to push the harmonium out of the song.

'The reason why subsequent recordings did not work was the lack of interaction. I believe the first one was better because of the emotional connect between the co-artistes and instrumentalists involved in the recording. Everybody was giving their best shot at the time. The magic could not be replicated with him singing by himself to a recorded track.'

But *Arth* gave Jagjit the chance to reach out beyond urban India, into every small town where it was released. The songs, written by Kaifi Azmi who seemed to know instinctively what mood and metre would suit the singer's voice best, became a rage. '*Jhuki jhuki si nazar beqarar hai ke nahin*' and '*Tum itna jo muskura rahe ho*' became instant hits, heard to this day, though '*Koyi yeh kaise bataye*' and '*Tu nahin toh zindagi mein*' also found their share of popularity.

The four songs of *Arth* were augmented by two more songs when the album was released in the market. Mahesh Bhatt, who produced and directed *Arth*, realized that Jagjit's suggestion was a valid one. The additional songs were written by Rajinder Nath 'Rehbar' and Iftikhar Imam Siddiqui, and set to music by Kuldeep Singh. Two more couplets were also added to '*Koi yeh kaise bataye*' in the cassette to get the playing time to the maximum duration.

Dovetailing *Arth* came another surprise film offer, *Saath Saath.*

Director Raman Kumar was making an offbeat film. Hoping for a certain kind of music, which would do justice to his gentle story, he approached Kuldeep Singh. Knowing too that screenplay writer Javed Akhtar, who had notched up a number of hits with partner Salim Khan but was now on the verge of breaking loose from the partnership, had inherited his father Jaan Nisar Akhtar's poetic talents, Raman Kumar approached him to write the lyrics. And he wanted Jagjit and Chitra to sing the songs of the film. 'Ever since I heard him sing Batalvi, I decided that if I ever made a film, Jagjit would sing in it,'

Jagjit with Kaifi Azmi, Shaukat Azmi and Jalal Agha

he told Kuldeep, and wondered if the now successful singer would be affordable. On Kuldeep's assurance, Raman approached Jagjit and Chitra for *Saath Saath.*

Resources were low. The film was funded by NFDC(National Film Development Corporation of India). But Jagjit, with characteristic generosity, did not discuss money. In fact, while working on the film, he would quietly pay for the food at times when the director was unable to do so. Raman was convinced that he also contributed towards the studio fees once the recordings were completed.

Kuldeep Singh, whose compositions for *Saath Saath* continue to sell even today, thirty-two years after the film's release, was more than happy to share memories of the making of the film. He narrated the story with gusto, adding how Jagjit agreed readily to sing for the film, with no talk of money. They had been younger and needier when they had first known each other, in the meetings outside Gaylord, and since then Jagjit had attained a fair measure of fame, but it was as if the years in between had never existed. Kuldeep Singh admitted that he approached Jagjit because he felt the singer's name on the credits would help sell both the film and the music.

He also shared a story that gives an insight into the singer's passion

Jagjit, the arranger of his own compositions

'AFTER THREE OR FOUR DAYS, JAGJIT SAID HE WANTED TO RE-RECORD THE SONG. HE BELIEVED HE HAD NOT GIVEN HIS BEST TO IT. I TOLD HIM THAT WAS NOT POSSIBLE. HE TRIED ANYWAY, DIFFERENT VERSIONS FOR THE NEXT FEW DAYS. I HELD MY PEACE, SAYING NOTHING. FINALLY, HE AGREED THAT THE FIRST VERSION WAS THE BEST. I REALIZED LATER, HE WAS TRYING TO PUSH THE HARMONIUM OUT OF THE SONG.'

VIDEO CASSETTE COVER OF *SAATH SAATH*

DOUBLE-ALBUM AUDIO CASSETTE COVER OF *SAATH SAATH* AND *ARTH*

for a good song. 'There was a song, '*Yeh bata de mujhe zindagi*', which was left out of the film. We decided there was no space or scene for it. Jagjit said to me, "This is the best song, let us record it for the album at least. I will arrange it myself." I confessed to him that I did not have so much money. He said it did not matter, he would do it for free, but the song could not be left out.'

Kuldeep remembers Jagjit's versatility as a singer. 'He would sing "*Mann dole*" from *Nagin* in many ways; at small functions, he would have the audience in splits as he sang it with Punjabi gusto, then as if a pujari were singing, then a pheriwala or a chowkidar. He would make it a complete entertainment item by itself.'

The songs of *Arth* were being recorded at Western Outdoor studio in South Bombay at the same time as the music of *Saath Saath.* Kuldeep often wondered how he could bring out the best in Jagjit's voice, without making music that sounded like the singer's own compositions. He had to work hard to this end. He remembers the recording of the still popular '*Yeh tera ghar, yeh mera ghar*'. 'His voice came out differently and he stopped singing to ask me to bring down the pitch. I hesitated. He was quiet for a moment, then said, "Okay, I will sing it the way you want."'

Saath Saath would earn Jagjit a lot of royalty. On meeting Kuldeep, he would ask if the composer had got his due from the music house. 'If I said no, he would say, "Get it in my name."' Kuldeep also gives Chitra full credit for being an apt pupil and singing exactly the way he envisaged the song.

In fact, such was the success of *Saath Saath* that Sanjeev Kohli decided to release a second version of the jacket for the album. The earlier one had Deepti Naval and Farooq Sheikh on it, the second had Chitra and Jagjit. The difference in sales was markedly in favour of the singers.

HMV's clever move to bring out a combined package of *Arth* and *Saath Saath* has earned rich rewards for all concerned. The double album is one of their highest-selling records, competing with the biggest soundtracks from all-time hit films.

JACKETS OF *THE UNFORGETTABLES* AND
FORGET ME NOT, WITH JAGJIT SINGING SOLO

Making a career move that would prove to be a turning point in his life, Kohli joined HMV in 1984. His track record must have impressed the leading music house to snap him up. Kohli saw the move as a means to work with the legendary names contracted with HMV, most of whom he had seen frequenting his father's home. From being a youngster who had sat on Lata-ji's lap when she worked with Madan Mohan, he was now a young man who would be recording her. Among the stars, of course, was Jagjit Singh as well.

At the time, HMV was allegedly underpaying its artistes. Jagjit was in dire financial straits still, despite *The Unforgettables* and his extensive tours. To get the price he felt he deserved, Jagjit was thinking of breaking his contract with HMV and shifting to T-Series, which was wooing the singer actively.

When Kohli planned to create a *khazana* of ghazals as he had done at Polydor, Jagjit refused to be a part of it. According to Kohli, 'Jagjit had created his own space and he was possessive about it as he had struggled a fair bit to get where he was. He was sure of his talent, and very critical of the less talented. He would not agree to any situation where he was likely to be clubbed with those he considered less talented than himself. The only time he agreed was when Ghulam Ali came to India and a session with Jagjit was planned.'

HMV, on the other hand, wanted to make the most of Jagjit's continued popularity. Kohli was told to record Jagjit more and more.

Working at full throttle to get the most out of Jagjit Singh, Kohli launched a new album, *A Milestone,* in which Jagjit and Chitra sang ghazals written by the iconic Pakistani poet, Qateel Shifai. A series of albums would follow, each hot on the heels of the other. The one that was considered the couple's best after *The Unforgettables* was titled *Ecstasies.* The playlist included eight ghazals: '*Jawan hai raat saqiya sharab la sharab la*', '*Pasine pasine hue ja rahe ho*', '*Tumne sooli pe latakte jise dekha hoga*', '*Mere jaise ban jaoge*', '*Jabse hum tabah ho gaye*', '*Humko dushman ki nigahon se*', '*Ek nazar dekh ke hum jaan gaye*' and '*Bahut dinon ki baat hai*'.

Kohli remembers, 'I had to do a lot of convincing to get Jagjit to sign up for another album. He had stopped recording with HMV by then. Somehow, because he saw me as Madan Mohan's son, and also realized that I was as passionate about my work as he was about his, he came around.' Meanwhile, things were changing at the music house too. 'The management changed, with the Goenkas taking over. They were in awe of most of the singers, Jagjit included, and that helped to boost the artistes' egos. I did my bit to change the atmosphere and make work enjoyable in the recording studios.'

Kohli realized that Jagjit Singh was a natural in the studio. 'It was a delight to record with him. He was not just a singer and composer. During recordings, he had the edge of being able to arrange his own music. He was technically very advanced, and very particular. He would do everything himself, and re-record until he felt the result was perfect. At times, he would also play the piano, or the accordion, or choose to play the harmonium or keyboard. The fact that he worked with a fixed set of musicians worked to his advantage. Not only did they have a perfect rapport, but the budgets were lower too.'

It was a quality that impressed all those Jagjit recorded with, including Daman Sood, who believed that he was unique in his ability to plan, record and perfect an album so that it was flawless in every aspect. He remembers Jagjit with grand affection. The very tone of his voice changes when he talks about the singer with whom he worked through the peak of his career. 'My association started soon after I met Jagjit for the first time. He had come to pick Chitra, who had just finished recording at Bombay Sound Services for Jaidev's *Do Hanson Ka Joda*. She had recorded a solo number, and I remember her in a white sari waiting after the recording, and Jagjit coming to pick her up.' By 1975, Sood and Jagjit had struck up a friendship. They would meet at Moti Mahal, near the HMV studios, to drink lassi and feast on the chole-puri that the restaurant was famous for. Jagjit was singing jingles then, and Sood would often be the recordist on the job. He remembers that Jagjit would always be dressed in jeans and bush shirt. 'We were recording *Forget Me Not* for a producer in Canada, and I can still picture Jagjit sitting on the floor and singing.'

Sood and Jagjit worked together on seventy-five albums in all. He remembers the last one, *Close To My Heart*, as one of his personal favourites. It has Jagjit singing songs originally sung by Hemant Kumar, Kishore Kumar and K.L. Saigal, and was his tribute to them. 'He would put in his own expressions without changing the melody. I would say, as a singer he sounded better than the original in doing this,' Sood avers.

A portrait of the singing couple

Perhaps what impressed Sood most was the dedication Jagjit Singh brought to his music. He was, according to the recordist, 'his own severest critic who would review his own singing. He would mix for three to four hours, then listen, cancel and redub. He wanted 100 per cent from himself'.

'There were songs he composed for Chitra, but which she never got around to singing after her withdrawal from music and public life. But he would never sing them. They had been composed for Chitra, and they would remain hers. His generosity made him offer the best songs from the lot to Lata Mangeshkar when he was planning *Sajda.* He wanted every artiste to give their best, and did what he could to ensure it by offering lyrics and tunes to suit their voice.'

And, of course, there was his voice that charmed everyone. As Nida Fazli put it, 'His voice has a strange magic; it is layered. We feel that he sings with a smile on his face, but within the words, he is weeping and making us weep. That is his amazing art. Jagjit's voice is a gift from God.'*

By the time *Ecstasies* was being recorded, Kohli remembers, 'Multi-track recording had begun. Jagjit and Chitra would record separately. When Chitra would come for her portions, she would lock the studio and then start recording.'

Passion ignites passion. A man of ideas, Kohli thought up ways to capitalize on the fact that Jagjit was ruling the music scene, so to say. 'He was doing a lot of concerts still, they were all packed houses. I said, "Let us launch an album at a concert, and let's promote it there. Let us name the concert after the album: 'Jagjit and Chitra Singh Present *Ecstasies*'." He agreed and it worked wonderfully. All the copies, released after the show, sold out.'

New ideas came in as the shows continued, sometimes rising out of a sticky situation. Kohli remembers the time when they were at a show in Jaipur. The chief guest was a minister, who was to launch the album, the show was based on, during the interval. Jagjit hated the whole idea of a chief guest, especially a politician, but he went along. The entire administration of the city was put on hold. When the minister sent word at the eleventh hour that he was unable to make it as his flight was delayed, Kohli admitted he was close to tears. 'It was one of my first marketing exercises; HMV had agreed with difficulty to let me go ahead with it, and I knew I would be pulled up for the failure. But Jagjit saved the day, and I will never forget that.

'When the curtain came down for the interval, the audience was restless with anticipation. Jagjit stepped off the stage, and saw the look of despair on my face. "What happened, why are you so *udaas*?" he asked. I told him the reason. The chief guest had not turned up. The audience was disappointed. Someone was bound to complain to the bosses at the headquarters. And though it was not my fault, I would have to take the flak. He was quick to respond. "Just write down A to Z on twenty-six pieces of paper. Then write one to twenty on twenty chits. We'll do a lucky draw." I was not sure what he was planning but complied. Seeing me puzzled, he explained, "We will pull out a number and a letter and do it with the audience watching. We will tell them that whoever is sitting in the seat whose number and row match

**The quote has been taken from the book* Beyond Time, *a limited edition published by Pankaj Kodesia & Associates in 2002*

with the number and letter we draw out, will inaugurate the show." It was sheer genius! It worked so well. The audience went wild. We repeated the idea, it became a ritual, and we never invited a chief guest again. Jagjit's presence of mind saved the day.'

Jagjit and Chitra would involve themselves in every aspect of record releases. Chitra would work on the names of the albums. Kohli recollects that as was the norm, he mainly chose Urdu names for the records he released at Polydor. However, Chitra had a liking for English names. When he wondered aloud what to name the new collection they had just recorded, Chitra said, '*Urdu wurdu mat rakho*, let us call it *Ecstasies*.' Jagjit would keep out of the debate. When asked about his view on the title, he replied from the corner he was sitting in, '*Ecstasies wekstasies kuch bhi rakho*, if it is in English, you decide.'

So the album was named *Ecstacies*. Neither Chitra nor Kohli, in their flurry, realized the name had been wrongly spelt. 'There was no such word in the dictionary and it confused everyone, especially in the design and production department,' Kohli remembers. 'The result was that when the album was released in the market, there was a discrepancy. While the label on the record said '*Ecstasies*', the jacket spelt it as '*Ecstacies*', with a 'c' instead of the 's'.

'The production department said it would take them another month to print and change the jackets. So we stacked up all the jackets and with paint added a curl to the 'c' to make it an 's'. Jagjit, ever the perfectionist, was livid.'

Around the time the recording of *A Sound Affair* started, Jagjit got interested in racing. He bought a few horses, which he would race, and he would be very excited about them. In fact, there was a point when his passion for racing almost threatened his very career.

Daman Sood remembers the time when, during the recording of

The corrected jacket of Ecstasies

With his beloved racehorses

AROUND THE TIME THE RECORDING OF *A SOUND AFFAIR* STARTED, JAGJIT GOT INTERESTED IN RACING. HE BOUGHT A FEW HORSES, WHICH HE WOULD RACE, AND HE WOULD BE VERY EXCITED ABOUT THEM. IN FACT, THERE WAS A POINT WHEN HIS PASSION FOR RACING ALMOST THREATENED HIS VERY CAREER.

A Sound Affair, Jagjit Singh lost his voice. 'He had been to the races and got very excited because his horse suddenly took the lead. He went berserk, shouting to egg it on, and when it won by what can only be called a fluke, he was over the moon. He kept shouting in excitement. When he woke up the next day, he had lost his voice. It took four months for him to get it back to singing form again.

'Of course, it worried him no end. He would ask me, "Will I never sing again?" his face tight with worry. He had to cancel all his shows for three months, and the recordings stopped.'

Sood remembers that it was Lata Mangeshkar who came to Jagjit's rescue. She told Sood it had happened to her too. Her voice would crack when carrying a tune, and she had suffered from the problem for six months before landing a medicine that helped her find her voice again. 'Tell him to call me,' Lata said, and soon Jagjit's voice was well on its way to being as good as new.

Despite this incident, Jagjit's love of horses and racing continued unabated. He would visit the race course regularly, speak with his jockeys, and ensure he kept up to date on the welfare of his horses.

When in 1985-86 *A Sound Affair* was released, Jagjit, on a whim, named one of his horses 'Sound Affair' too. 'You keep choosing English names for my albums that I don't quite understand,' he would say laughingly to Sood, 'I will name my horses the same.'

If there was anything that rankled about the albums he recorded with Jagjit and Chitra Singh, it was the fact that in the studio Jagjit would brook no interference. Even suggestions were not entertained. Sanjeev Kohli found it an unwelcome departure, for 'even when Lata or Rafi were recording, I would be able to share my inputs'.

While Jagjit preferred to release one album every two years, believing that it was good to make the audience thirst for them, HMV was dismayed by the fact that the younger newcomers were heaping releases one on top of the other in a bid to get a share of the market. Kohli had to convince his star that they needed to keep pace. Jagjit also had to realize that marketing the releases was important, and though he still fought shy of shows exclusively for the press, he allowed them to attend his launch events.

Things were going smoothly. HMV and Jagjit Singh had worked out an arrangement, which would keep the fans reaching out to buy new releases at regular intervals year after year. Jagjit had already set the benchmark in contemporizing the ghazal, using instruments never used before. His technique of arranging and recording set the standard. 'Listen to Jagjit Singh and create such an album' was often a whisper heard floating down the corridors of music houses. In 1986, *Echoes* was recorded. All should have been quiet and easy but for one small hitch. Jagjit Singh wanted to try something different.

He came up with a plan that threw HMV into utter confusion.

HMV had meanwhile managed to capture two other ghazal giants on tape. Ghulam Ali and Mehdi Hassan had toured India from Pakistan. There were no audio cassettes available to offer to their fans, no radio interviews were permitted, so there was no exposure to that medium either. Moving swiftly, the music company recorded them live, and released their albums into the market: *The Latest, The Best: Ghazals from Ghulam Ali, The Best of Ghulam Ali, Jashn-E-Bahar, Ghulam Ali Live in Concert Vols. I and II* and *The Finest Ghazals of Mehdi Hassan.*

The compilations were huge hits. Ghazal lovers, awakening to the charms of the new format and the fresh new voices and singing styles, took to the releases, making them superhits.

While the sales proved that both singers had their niche fan following in India too, the fact remained that Jagjit Singh still stood towering above them.

When, in 1987, Jagjit Singh, bored with what he had now mastered, hit upon the idea of recording an album abroad, Kohli was willing to go along. The idea appealed to the adventurer in both men.

Recording overseas would deliver a new level of sound quality that could improve sales figures manifold and have a domino effect on past

Covers of A Sound Affair *and compilations by Mehdi Hassan and Ghulam Ali. HMV's coup.*

A gesture of humility: with Mehdi Hassan

releases by capturing new, younger audiences. But the idea proved to be easier said than done. Kohli recollects, 'It was tough to convince the bosses. They wanted to know why we needed to go overseas; where the money was going to come from; how a healthy bottom line would be viable. If Jagjit's recordings sold so well when recorded in India, what was the need to go abroad? I explained that we could enhance sound quality, expand our audience base and also create a CD. Finally, with much reluctance, the go-ahead was granted.'

A recce trip to London followed. Jagjit wanted a studio in London that would not charge by the hour. He wanted a twenty-four hour space as he was taking his musicians along too. Jacob's Studio, about 100 kilometres away from London, was found suitable and booked for fifteen days. Two engineers were put in attendance on twelve-hour shifts.

Kohli remembers the madness of the period. 'Days of frenzied activity followed. We lived there, food was cooked on the premises, with Chitra supervising the cooking. The atmosphere was fantastic, charged as it was with creativity. Since Jagjit was also the arranger, he wrote out the scores for all the musicians. The Brits were amazed. How, they wondered, could there be a man who composed, sang, arranged, played instruments and handled engineering, fine-tuning, all by himself!'

Almost fifteen ghazals were recorded, with Chitra singing some solos besides the duets. *Beyond Time* included some numbers that have gone down in history as among the best loved songs: '*Apni aankhon ke samundar mein utar jaane de*', '*Jhoothi sachchi aas pe jeena kab tak aakhir aakhir kab tak*', '*Log har mod pe ruk ruk ke sambhalte kyun hain*', '*Mera dil bhi shauq se todo*', among others.

Once the recording was complete, the team returned to India. Jagjit Singh carried the mixed master tape with him.

But the story was not to end there. When he listened to the master tape on his return, Jagjit realized something was not quite right. It soon dawned on him that the engineers had got the mixing wrong.

Explaining the problem he said, 'The engineers there are Western, with their own ideas of sound; their approach is to keep the voice level low. Our engineers understand that in the ghazal the words are important and should be heard. So I went to London again, and recalled the files from the computer so that I could do the mixing again to my standard. Each song was re-balanced. When the album was released, it was a totally different hearing experience.'

But the problems were not over yet. The songs recorded totalled seventy instead of the ninety minutes required for an audio cassette. It meant dropping two songs or adding two more. Kohli decided to add songs to the cassette but keep the CD as is. Sood remembers the story clearly. 'In fact, when Jagjit asked me to take on the task of adding the songs, I was hesitant. I said we would never get a perfect match, there was bound to be a noticeable difference, if not a drop in recording quality. "Take your musicians and go back to London and do it there," I advised. He looked at me for a long while, then said softly in Punjabi, "If you want, you can do it. You are Daman Sood." "Okay, let's take a shot at it," I said, enthused. The fact that I had the best equipment added to my new-found confidence. I asked him to sing, and tried to match the voice exactly. It worked. He was pleased. In fact, the only clue to telling which songs were recorded here is the fact that the ones done here have the sitar added to the ensemble.' *Beyond Time* is still a benchmark, with highly experienced sound engineers using the CD as a reference for balancing sound at a concert of Indian music.

As always, Chitra Singh worked closely on the title and look of the album, and rising to the occasion, HMV organized a function where all the music greats gathered to welcome the latest advancement in their world of music.

Sood has countless memories of working with Jagjit, all of which he holds very dear, including an account of a typical working day. The scene he sketches is easy to visualize: Jagjit Singh walking into the recording studio at around 10 a.m. Raising a hand in greeting, or sometimes greeting Sood with a hug, he would settle down and pick up his diary and betting papers that would give him the information he required about the day's races. He would look up briefly and say 'track lagao', and listen to it as it played in the background. By noon, he would be done with his racing papers and phone calls. By 12.30 p.m., he would call out to Sood busy with his work. 'Let's eat,' he would say. After lunch, he would stretch out on the couch, and soon fall asleep. Around 2.30 p.m., he would sit up, and Sood knew that his working day had begun. He would go on, often until 9 or 9.30 in the night, totally absorbed in his music.

Over the years, Sood and Jagjit forged a bond of friendship that sealed their working partnership. Sood would get insights into the nature of the singer during their travels. 'He had a unique way of arguing to his own advantage,' Sood remembers with affection. 'He would argue with me over his smoking. I would not allow cigarettes in the control room. He would get anxious for a smoke and fight with me, citing Gulzar and Talat Mahmood as examples of how smoking added to the timbre of a voice. He tried to persuade

With Pandit Shiv Kumar Sharma

me that smoking would actually improve his voice by adding resonance to his bass notes.' Of course, once he had his first heart attack, when he was performing at Oswals in Ludhiana, he was forced to give up smoking. 'Jagjit was also forced to give up his other habit due to the heart attack—of having a bit of rum in a steel glass to warm up his throat.'

Sood accompanied Jagjit on almost all his overseas tours, not just because he was so good in balancing sound exactly as the musician wanted it, but also because Jagjit trusted him to ensure none of the shows were secretly recorded. 'He was so popular; it was a huge and very real risk.'

On such trips, Jagjit would often surprise Sood by waking him up with a cup of bed tea, or ironing his suit for him, saying, 'because, anyway I am ironing my own kurta'. Sood would sometimes be surprised by the sight of Jagjit making sherbet or tea for them all despite Chitra's presence in the same room. Perhaps one of the reasons why Sood believes he owes so much to Jagjit is that the singer helped hone his skills. 'While we were working on *Beyond Time*, I watched him closely. He was the best editor I have ever seen. He would edit in such a way that the music would take on a wonderful new quality. I learnt editing from him, learnt how to infuse soul into the final tape. In Jagjit's hands, the instruments would gain a soulful edge, and his editing brought the emotional quotient of his singing to the fore.'

It was at Jagjit's insistence alone that Sood first worked on a 24-track recorder. 'If I get it, will you work on it?' he had asked Sood. He had convinced the owners of the Nanavati Studio in Bombay to import and install the recording device, which cost about twenty-four lakhs after duties. 'He handled the entire process of making challans and indenting for the purchase,' Sood remembers with fondness.

FATHER AND SON IN CANADA

The years ahead brought tremendous changes. On the music front, technology was fast evolving. Digital recording became the norm in India. Jagjit, bored with the long stints at recording studios, declared that he was not willing to spend big chunks of time creating albums. Instead, he would record a song whenever he felt it was ready, and store it, adding to the stock till there were enough numbers to put together under a title in a CD. He told HMV they could pay him as and when a recording was scheduled.

If the music company felt the idea was audacious, they had no option but to comply. Jagjit and Chitra Singh had become too big a label to argue with. Star airs were somewhat inevitable with star status, and he was the ghazal's biggest star.

Soon after *Beyond Time*, Kohli shifted to London. Busy with new assignments over there, his contact with the Singhs was at best sporadic.

Meanwhile, though their career was soaring, and money was pouring in, as were accolades and invitations, and even though the Singhs were now moving in high circles and interacting with famous stars, they were suddenly about to become lonely.

In 1987, while on a trip to the US with his parents, Baboo dropped a bombshell. He wanted to stay back. Chitra and Jagjit were shocked. They couldn't imagine a single day without their son around. But seeing his eagerness, they agreed. It would be for a short while, they told themselves. Little did they know what the future held for them.

Among their most ardent fans was one K.D. Kapoor, who lived in the US. He was crazy enough to track Jagjit's concerts across the world, attending every single one, be it in Holland, Canada or England. Their friendship had grown, and was now almost two decades old. And when they were touring the US in 1987, the Singhs visited the Kapoor home in Hudson, Ohio. They were friendly enough to trust their hosts with their most precious belonging, and left Baboo with them for the two months of their tour, so he could join a local school and stay in touch with his studies.

When it was time to return to India, and Chitra and Jagjit went to pick him up, Baboo begged to stay on. The Kapoors were also delighted with the idea; their children had already left home and they were lonely.

Chitra agrees now, that one year in the US was a wonderful experience for Baboo. The boy who studied with reluctance, that too just before

Happy threesome: Chitra with Monica and Vivek

the exams, suddenly changed. His results shot up. He loved the system there and the fact that he got recognition on his own merit. It transformed him completely from a child into a confident young man. It was also a freedom of sorts for the Singhs, who did not have to worry about his being alone while they spent evening after evening at performances and after-parties. 'We knew he was happy, and it made us feel no guilt about the fact that our lives had got busier and we had no time for him. We were delighted with his new persona when he returned. As his visa could not be extended, he had to remain in India, and he enrolled at Sydenham College, Bombay.'

At Sydenham College, the young man became as popular as his father had been in his own college. Whether it was football, tennis, cricket or a party, it was considered incomplete without Baboo. Inheriting his father's ease and ability to mix with everyone, and blessed with good looks from both his parents, Baboo soon became the captain of the college cricket team, and seemed all set to shine in sports even after completing his studies.

His love for music remained. He developed a critical faculty, and would listen and comment on his father's compositions while they were being created, pointing out anything that did not seem to appeal instantly, or fell short of his father's high level of creativity.

Around this time, Chitra fell ill.

'In 1984, I started suffering from unbearable headaches, which doctors and I believed were migraines. I would suffer non-stop, sometimes for ten days at a stretch. I would go to bed hoping to sleep, but wake up with it still hammering away at me inside. My ex-husband got me some medicine, which would numb the pain for an hour or two. Soon I became dependent on it. I also learned to smoke, as it dulled the pain. Dutta was a chain smoker, and I caught the habit.'

The pain began radiating upwards, and soon Chitra could not turn her head. Finally, her daughter came to her aid. 'Monica had given me the number of a neurologist, Dr Keki Turell, who had cured her friend's mother of a tumour at the base of her brain by neatly scooping it out. I accompanied a friend,

With Sagoo, a friend from Toronto

MOTHER AND SON. VIVEK NURSED CHITRA
THROUGH HER ILLNESS AND SURGERY.

Ramesh Mehra, whose son needed a consultation, to Dr Turell's clinic. In the waiting room, the doctor saw me sitting holding my neck and asked what the matter was. I told him, and he was immediately on high alert.'

The doctor was very flattered to be consulted by the stellar Chitra Singh, a fact that she found extremely flattering too. He asked her a lot of questions, and asked for some X-rays to be taken. Chitra wanted to know why a neurosurgeon was giving her advice, and he retorted that it was not advice but an order.

'So I went back to him with the X-rays, and he placed them in a row, then took out a skeleton and, placing it alongside, asked me to see the difference. I told him there was no space between my vertebrae. He said I would have to undergo a surgical procedure. He would insert acrylic liquid which would take shape to make space, and then he would implant new discs in place of the pulverized discs. I consulted Jagjit, and he, in his usual manner, said, "Dekh le". So I went ahead.'

'The surgery was complicated. To avoid accident, and also because of calcification and osteoarthritic deposits and the need to manipulate the vertebrae, Dr Turell wanted to cut in from the front. The nerve centres at the back were at the risk of being ripped, which could have resulted in paralysis. There was also the risk in the frontal approach of the vocal chords being hurt. It was a tough choice, but he felt the front was a safer option.'

The operation lasted ten hours, and Chitra was sentenced to two months in bed, with a high collar to hold the neck in place. All through this time, Vivek looked after her. He was caring, and would take care of his grandmother too, whenever she needed help.

The two months passed slowly. 'I was not allowed to move, or talk or sing, and when the collar came off and I tried to sing, I found the vertical muscles too weak. My voice was never quite the same afterwards, but my performance improved slowly, and thanks to experience and maturity, I learned to handle my voice properly. I started recording again.'

KINDRED SOULS: JAGJIT AND GULZAR

Despite these ups and downs, the 1980s would end on a high note, with Jagjit and Chitra singing for Gulzar's TV serial, *Mirza Ghalib.*

When Gulzar decided to make *Mirza Ghalib* for television, his first and only choice for the music was Jagjit Singh. Gulzar believes that three people were involved closely in the making of the serial, 'Jagjit Singh, Naseeruddin Shah and no, not me, but Mirza Ghalib!'

When Gulzar approached Jagjit for the music of the serial, the two sat down to decide where the songs would be placed. Chitra was not involved at this point. She became close to Gulzar much after *Mirza Ghalib* was completed. They found common ground to share, based on the fact that she was Bengali. 'Gulzar likes Bengalis,' as Chitra puts it.

According to Jagjit, 'The ghazals were selected according to the narrative. Some were done in *mushaira* style, some in *kotha* style, and some in *faqir* style: Gulzar wanted to show how Ghalib became popular. So we discussed what the situation was, and what the treatment should be. Over half the songs were composed in the studio and recorded there.'

Jagjit composed the rest of the songs mostly by himself, at home. Gulzar would give him a scene, a mood or a situation, and he would take it away, mull over it and come back with a first draft. There would be no notations, Gulzar would realize, just the tune for his approval. Some of the music was composed, after discussion, right there at Gulzar's house.

Jacket of the soundtrack of the hit television series Mirza Ghalib

Celebration time: Tanvi Azmi, Sushila R.P. Goenka (then chairman's wife) and V.K. Dubey of HMV with Chitra, Jagjit and Gulzar

WHEN GULZAR DECIDED TO MAKE *MIRZA GHALIB* FOR TELEVISION, HIS FIRST AND ONLY CHOICE FOR THE MUSIC WAS JAGJIT SINGH. GULZAR BELIEVES THAT THREE PEOPLE WERE INVOLVED CLOSELY IN THE MAKING OF THE SERIAL, 'JAGJIT SINGH, NASEERUDDIN SHAH AND NO, NOT ME, BUT MIRZA GHALIB!'

The entire process of making the serial, complete with music, spanned more than a year. Part of the reason, Gulzar explained, was that it was a complex musical project. 'I did not allow Jagjit to use any instrument that did not exist at that time. And it led to clashes between us. He would say, "Where is the space for composition then?" He would not be prepared to give up his electronics. He also rejected the idea of making an album of the music, saying it was pointless without the instruments he wanted.'

Jagjit also felt challenged by the fact that every singer, from Talat and Lata to Begum Akhtar, Mehdi Hassan and Suraiya, had sung Ghalib. He had to be different.

'The singing had to be straightforward. Ghalib was a poet, not a singer, so there was no place for complicated musical taans. He would have recited the poetry, so I kept the music simple with a few variations. I never felt that this is Jagjit Singh composing for *Mirza Ghalib*, so I must display my musical virtuosity. No, it should be Ghalib. Jagjit Singh should become Ghalib and sing, only then will the poetry come forth.' The result of this introspection on Jagjit's part was that Gulzar went on record saying in high praise that, '*Mirza Ghalib* is Jagjit beyond Jagjit.'

Chitra shares a funny story about the serial. 'Maybe it was after the third episode was aired, a male voice came on the telephone line asking if it was Jagjit Singh's house. I said yes, and he said he wanted to speak to him. I asked if I could take a message and he responded that he had no message. "I just wanted to ask him, a*chcha bhala chal raha tha*, female voice *ghusane ki kya zaroorat thi*?"'

Determined to make an album of Mirza Ghalib's songs even though Jagjit was against it, Gulzar approached the sound recordist at Western Outdoor studios where the recordings had been done, telling him that he would buy the two-inch tapes, and that he should not erase them.

Once the serial went off the air, Gulzar asked Jagjit if he would fill in the tracks with instruments as he wanted. Jagjit wanted to know what would come of it. 'I will pay you more for it,' Gulzar said. 'I cannot ask anyone else to do it.' Jagjit started work, filling the tape in with sarod and other instruments so that it was not *nanga* as he had termed it in its original form.

Gulzar said, 'Jagjit got very enthused, he arranged it as if touched by inspiration. It was a dramatic change. He made history with that album.'

More felicitations for Mirza Ghalib

The two creative men shared a deep understanding of each other's work and genius. According to the poet, 'Jagjit was younger, but he would scold me. He'd say, "Give me a *sher* that will touch my heart," and I would respond with, "I try hard, but it does not reach your heart. *Nishana chook jata hai.*"' The link between them remained strong.

They collaborated on other albums later in their lives, and also did stage shows together on the ghazal theme to the delight of audiences who were fans of both men. They even got together for a musical series tracing the path and history of the ghazal, which Kohli recorded for HMV, first as cassettes and then as CDs. *The Collectors' Special* had songs by Noor Jehan and Saigal as well as Jagjit and Chitra Singh and other contemporary ghazal singers.

Mirza Ghalib set Jagjit on a new level. Though he composed the music for another TV serial, *Kahkashan*, in 1991-'92, written by no less a writer than Ali Sardar Jafri, on the lives of six great Urdu poets: Hasrat Mohani, Jigar Moradabadi, Josh Malihabadi, Majaz Lucknawi, Firaq Gorakhpuri and Makhdoom Mohiuddin, and directed by Jalal Agha, he did not scale the heights he reached with *Mirza Ghalib* in those compositions.

Jazbe junoon ne aaj to gul hi naya khila diya
Khud woh gale se lipat gaye, ishq ka vaasta diya

Tu rahe tera gham rahe, main rahoon mera dam rahe
Kaun tujhe bula saka, kisne tujhe bhula diya

Mere hujoom-e-shauq par munh se to kuchh na keh sake
Chehre pe rang aa gaya, haath mera daba diya

VIVEK SINGH BEING CHEEKY

The year 1990, which started off like any other, would, by July, bring with it an incident that would change the lives of Jagjit and Chitra forever.

Music continued to flow, shows were plentiful. A bunch of young talent looked up to Jagjit Singh as their mentor, sponsor or patron.

At home, the joy of having a close-knit family made everything more meaningful. When Jagjit was not deeply immersed in composing, he would spend time with Baboo. If the boy was a grown-up now, moving in his own circles, and Jagjit sometimes felt he was not seeing enough of him, it was only a passing mood. He was after all a young man now, in his late teens, and needed to make his own life and group of friends.

Chitra remembers that her son was exactly like his father when it came to generosity. The stories about Jagjit Singh's unstintingly giving nature whenever he encountered someone in need are legion. Anyone who knew him was aware of this trait of his, and many whom he hardly knew but helped will readily share their story as a tribute to the singer.

Vivek Singh too would show the same empathy. 'He would drive around in his Gypsy, and stop en route to offer rides to anyone who

In a pensive mood

WITH LATA MANGESHKAR AT A FORMAL SHOOT FOR *SAJDA*

THE ALBUM JACKET, RELEASED WITH GREAT FANFARE

seemed to be waiting for a taxi or bus,' Chitra recalls. 'He would take everyone under his wing. There was a boy, lanky, all legs and arms, very tall, I think he must have been 6'3" at least. He was a baniya's son, and no one would talk to him, though he hung around. Baboo noticed this and got him into his group, ensuring everybody involved him in whatever they were doing.'

Baboo also introduced Chitra to pop music. 'He would play U2 and others, and I acquired a taste for the music. Dutta had inculcated a love of Western classical symphonies in me, and I loved Chopin, but my tastes widened, thanks to my son. He was my guru in many ways, my strength too. I have learnt so much from both my children. I am who I am thanks to whatever I have learnt from them.'

Talking of the father-son relationship, Chitra is clear that, 'Vivek Singh was Jagjit's world. He no longer had his paternal family around; his new creation was his entire world. We were both totally engrossed in our son, even Mini took a backseat. As he grew up, he spent less and less time with us, but one could sense that, as far as Jagjit was concerned, Baboo was the apple of his eye. If there was anything Jagjit thought of as entirely his own, it was his son, an extension of himself.'

One of Jagjit Singh's dearest wishes was to make an album with Lata Mangeshkar. Sanjeev Kohli remembers the day that Jagjit mentioned his secret desire to him, sometime in 1988, and requested him to approach Lata Mangeshkar, whom he knew because of Madan Mohan, his father.

Lata was not interested, asking why she should sing non-film songs for Jagjit Singh, though she did admire him as a singer. Besides, she wanted to sing only for composers she had a tuning with.

It would take two years for Lata to be convinced and agree to the album. If Lata had any doubts that the tuning with Jagjit would happen, they vanished as soon as she heard the songs. Jagjit was as frank as always. Kohli remembers that he came out of that meeting with Lata with flying colours, telling her that he had composed the songs over fifteen years and saved them for her to sing. 'I used jokes to break the ice; both Jagjit and Lata share a terrific sense of humour and a great repertoire of jokes, so we'd often begin each sitting with half an hour of joking around.' Once or twice, Vivek Singh also accompanied his father to these sittings.

MOMENTS WITH HIMSELF: JAGJIT WORKING OUT A TUNE

Where he made music

Though the recordings were fixed and the studios booked, progress on *Sajda* was slow. Kohli had moved to London on a two-year assignment, and Lata kept indifferent health, which caused frequent cancellations. Chitra, however, believed they were just star *nakhras*, but her husband, patient as ever, never lost his cool or his hope of seeing the album through. Kohli would intervene to help whenever he was in Bombay. He also suggested that Jagjit add a few of his own ghazals as well as a few duets, not just because that was what the audience would expect from the album, but also because with Lata's bouts of ill-health, chances were that the sixteen songs demanded of the double album would never get done.

Jagjit complied. Perennial favourites in *Sajda* like '*Har taraf har jagah*' and '*Gham ka khazana*' were woven in as duets. Jagjit's unforgettable solos included '*Tujh se milne ki saza*', which he often sang at concerts.

When Kohli took the rough cut of the songs recorded to Chitra, she listened carefully and said, '*Lata achcha nahin gaayeen... awaaz gayee.*'

Even as Jagjit Singh's dream of the joint album with the nation's most popular and revered female voice neared realization, his world came crashing down around him.

Sajda would not be released till January 1992.

APPLE OF HIS FATHER'S EYE: VIVEK SINGH

In 1992, a new album of Chitra and Jagjit Singh was released. It pre-dated *Sajda* and was called *Someone Somewhere.* The album had only eight songs. Unlike most of their earlier albums, this one did not have Jagjit and Chitra on the cover. It was a mysterious cover, with a pair of eyes looking at the potential listener.

'It was an unusual idea for a cover. I had to coax HMV for a long time before they agreed on using the design,' Kohli recollects. 'The risk was huge, because the album had no logo, nor names of the singers on the cover. All that information had to be conveyed through publicity alone.'

Despite this, the album sold well. It had been two years since the Singhs had released an album into the market, and as Jagjit had predicted, the silence had indeed stoked the thirst of the public for something new from the ghazal king. The dealers did their bit, pushing the album through instore publicity. The public lapped it up.

Perhaps the thought that this could be the last of the releases by Jagjit and Chitra also motivated HMV on one hand to bend its rules on covers, and the public, on the other hand, to pick up copies as soon as they hit the stores. In fact, that might as well have been true.

But for a desire to bring out a music collection as a tribute to their son, *Someone Somewhere* might never have been released.

The Singhs were in deep mourning. This was the first indication to the music world that at least one of them was willing to face the world again, after the long silence that overtook them in July 1990.

Chitra Singh will never forget the night of 28 July 1990. It was the night the Singh family's life, as they had known it until then, changed irrevocably. Never to be the same again.

Chitra recalls the night and its aftermath in photographic detail. 'That night, Papa was singing, I think it was at Anju Mahendru's party. I was at home, nursing a viral. Anyway, I was probably not invited; that happened quite frequently. Jehangir and Mini (Monica) were with us that time as their son, Armaan, was only nine months old. My mother was with the night nurse in her room.

'When the phone rang, it was the police. They said Baboo was in hospital, could we please come. I felt my heart clutching in fear. I woke Jehangir up, and tried calling Jagjit. We could not trace where he was, there were no mobile phones back then, of course. I quickly gave Jehangir some money and sent him off.

'Within minutes of Jehangir's going, the doorbell rang. "Get ready, we will take you," said some of Baboo's friends. We got ready, Mini and I, as quickly as my trembling hands would allow me to. We bundled the sleeping Armaan and took him with us to the hospital. We were too late. Baboo had left us forever.

'Jehangir kept calling the house repeatedly. Finally, at about five a.m., Jagjit picked up the phone.

'When he reached the hospital and came to know that Baboo was gone, he crashed. The nurse inside heard him falling and rushed out to help. He revived. After that it was him and his son. He looked at me, through me, as if I was of no consequence. Then he just pushed me aside, as if I did not exist, and entered the room where Baboo lay. I felt very hurt. I was the mother, I was shattered too, but I felt then that Papa thought my job was done after I produced a son for him. After that it was him and the boy. And now that the boy was gone, I did not exist.'

In *Beyond Time,** Jagjit Singh traced the fateful day's events as he experienced them. 'That evening, I was doing the background music for a Punjabi film. After that, I went to perform at a small concert arranged by Abdul Rehman Bukhatir of Dubai who was in town at the time. I finished the concert at about two in the morning and came home. I was changing my clothes when the call came. Chitra and the others were already at the hospital. The call was from Monica's husband, Jehangir. "There's been an accident," he said.

'"What happened?" I asked, "How is Baboo?" He told me, "He is no more."

'That was that. I got it straight, no beating about the bush. It was a moment of pure desperation, though I composed myself as soon as I could: a man can go to any lengths in his desperation. I still remember that in my haste, I wore my pyjamas inside out.'

Vivek Singh was eighteen years old, a month away from his nineteenth birthday, when he met with a road accident.

Road accidents happen all the time, but when a celebrity is involved even indirectly, it makes news. The newspapers were full of the story of Vivek's death, and the reports hung on the usual pegs: rich, spoilt kid, party scene, alcohol, etc.

As it happened, Vivek and two other boys—Sairaj Bahutule, a close friend and fellow cricket player who went on to play Ranji Trophy and become a legspinner, and

**Jagjit Singh's quotes have been taken from the book* Beyond Time, *a limited edition published by Pankaj Kodesia & Associates in 2002*

They were a close-knit threesome

Rahul Mazumdar—were driving down Marine Drive. Chances are that the car was travelling at high speed; the occupants were young, it was after 2 a.m. and the roads were empty. By the time Vivek, who was at the wheel, noticed the black ladder-like contraption that the municipality uses to fix the street lights standing at the extreme right, in the fast lane and next to the divider, the car had crashed into it. The accident killed Vivek Singh and seriously injured Sairaj and Rahul, who, however, recovered in due course of time.

With her mother and father in shock, unable to come to terms with their profound grief, it was Monica who took up cudgels for her dead brother. She felt what the press did to him was very unfair. He had died within minutes of the accident, at 2.49 a.m., but by morning his story was splashed across the pages, and Monica found the reports hurtful and defamatory. The forensic report came only eight months later, the papers had no basis for their maligning deductions about the cause of the accident. 'I fought single-handedly, going to Azad Maidan every day, dealing with the legalities. I went through Marine Drive getting affidavits

LOST IN THOUGHTS OF THE PAST.
JAGJIT NEVER GOT OVER THE LOSS OF HIS SON.

from residents. In the end, I cleared Baboo's name and got retractions. It was the least I could do. My parents were in no state to do that; actually, neither was I, but I had to be strong,' she had said in an interview given for *Beyond Time.**

Monica put her baby in a day care and went about doggedly till Vivek's name was cleared. Perhaps her efforts shamed the press and the authorities who were indeed responsible for an act of extreme negligence that allowed a dark, unmarked vehicle to be parked in the fast lane of a thoroughfare. They later gave in to Chitra's demand that the lane leading to their house, and connecting two important, arterial roads in South Bombay be named after Vivek Singh. A name that it holds till today.

Vivek's death shrouded the Singh house in silence. The music he had loved, and grown up on, was stilled. Chitra, in shock, retreated into a shell, barely speaking to anyone. Jagjit, equally devastated, moped around the house, and would not look at his beloved music. It was as if he had been betrayed by life itself.

'I could not face people, I would run inside. Baboo was like another firstborn, I had done everything for him from birth onwards. In Monica's case, my mother had taken care of her. I could not cope with losing him,' says Chitra. In a way, the Singhs leant on each other in this moment of grief, but something had been damaged irrevocably. 'The involvement was stronger after the accident, but he somehow withdrew from me. There was no sharing as before,' she says about Jagjit.

'He made many, many friends outside, as if he was looking for Baboo in every single young man. Often he would be exploited for this weakness. Papa became very lonely. The one thing in the world that was *his* was gone. It was like losing his very life.'

For six months, Jagjit Singh could not look beyond his grief. But his passion for music and Monica and her children woke him to an awareness of life. However, Chitra could not be reached in any manner.

After some weeks, Jagjit picked up his tanpura. He would strum it for hours, finding some solace in the sound. It was as if the notes were filtering through the layers of pain to move his heart once again.

'I felt I should not let what had happened become a weakness and crush me; instead I should turn it into a strength. In some quarters, it was being said that I was finished. These rumours made me even more determined,' Jagjit explained.

**Monica's quotes have been taken from the book* Beyond Time, *a limited edition published by Pankaj Kodesia & Associates in 2002*

A MOMENT FROM HAPPIER DAYS WHILE ON TOUR.
CHITRA STOPPED SINGING AFTER VIVEK'S DEATH.

The tanpura became his route to a meditative calm. 'Destiny stole our child from us. After Baboo's death, Chitra give up singing. She looked for Baboo in spirituality, I looked for him in my music.'* The memories, the pain and the tears were all there, but he drew them into himself, and held them back with the strength that music gave him. No one witnessed his anguish, except at the rare moments when during a concert, even years later, the dam would burst and his suppressed grief would give way to tears. A couplet, a word, anything would suddenly link him back to his loss, the wall of his forbearance would crumble, and he would break down, sometimes losing control, completely.

Six months after Baboo's death, he entered the living world again with a concert. His fans saw a Jagjit Singh they had not witnessed before, wounded as he was and still hurting. Two years later, when Kohli returned from the UK, Jagjit expressed a desire to release an album in his son's memory. He offered eight songs recorded by Chitra and himself some time ago, saying he wanted Vivek Singh on the cover. After much discussion with HMV, the album *Someone Somewhere* was released. 'I don't know if he would have approved of all the songs,' Jagjit would say about the playlist, keeping in mind that in recent years, his son had been his keenest critic.

Kohli, knowing that Jagjit needed emotional support, also helped coordinate the slow moving *Sajda* every time he visited India. He would persuade Lata to find time for the album saying it would help lift Jagjit out of his depression. Finally, in 1992, the double album was ready for release. The costs had spiralled, but it was a coup of unforgettable dimensions to have four duets with Lata and Jagjit, four solos by him and eight by Lata Mangeshkar.

'I planned an impressive function for the release,' Kohli remembers. 'Lata-ji suggested that Chitra come to the event to release the album. She came in white, looking like a shadow of her former self. The function was held at the Leela near the international airport in Bombay.'

The album proved to be a hit. But that did little to gladden the heart of either Jagjit or Chitra Singh.

Even as she grappled with her own bereavement, Monica helped her parents cope with their loss in yet another manner, besides clearing her brother's name. Being a psychic, she helped them reach out to Vivek spiritually.

**The quotes has been taken from* 'Unforgettable Moments with Jagjit Singh', Bombay Times, TNN, 10 November 2002

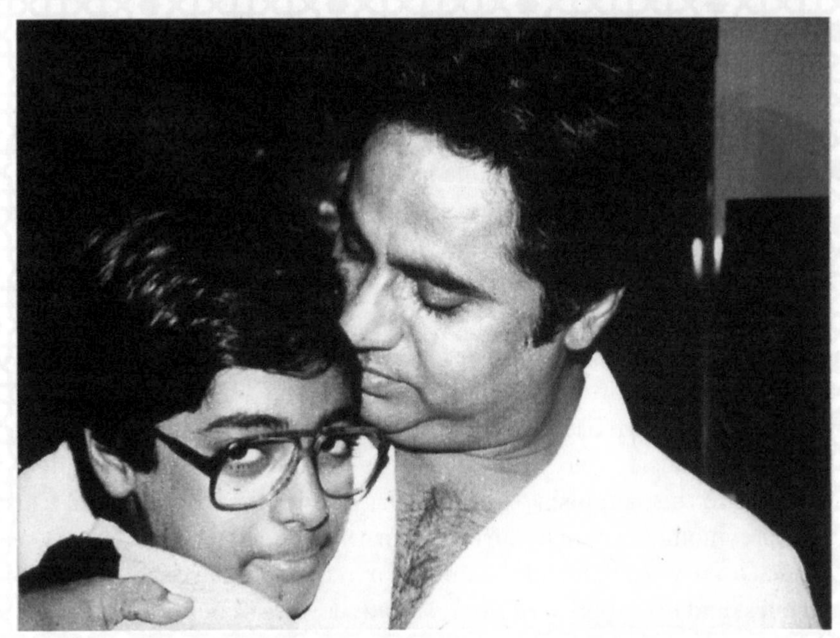

HAUNTED BY MEMORIES

23

Vivek's loss was a wedge in what had been a close marital relationship. After his death, it seemed as if Jagjit and Chitra chose completely different ways to deal with their grief.

The history of relationships is full of such stories. Chitra wondered if Papa held her responsible in some way. Perhaps he needed to attribute guilt to someone, to help himself deal better with the accident.

They had a place in Khandala. It had been bought in the mid 1980s and made habitable by 1988, and the family often went there for breaks. 'When the Kapoors of Ohio heard of Vivek's death, Mr Kapoor came down. Papa took him to Khandala. Mr Kapoor returned after a few days and was talking to me, when he asked me, "Do you think Jagjit blames you?" I was flabbergasted, and asked him if Papa had said anything. But, of course, Kapoor said nothing beyond that question. It left me wondering.'

However, the caring side of Jagjit never let Chitra down. She remembers him always by her side when she had to go out, his arm around her shoulders in a protective gesture. He understood what she was going through, but he had chosen his path, and it would lead him away from her. Chitra had given up singing, and he was finding it again. Though she could not help him, Chitra realized that he was alone.

She was fighting her own battles of faith, questioning why the tragedy befell them. Seeking answers, she combed the bookstores for books on spirituality, on communicating with those who had passed beyond and on philosophy.

Jagjit, seeking his way to return to some semblance of life, took up every programme offered to him. It was as if he could not bear to be at home with Baboo's memories around him. He took to drinking more, and started going more often to the races. Chitra heard that he was drinking more than he should, and in mixed company. 'I asked a friend to keep an eye on him, so he would be safe, and not fall into bad hands, but Jagjit, when he heard about it by accident, was wild, and took umbrage at the *jasoosi*.' There seemed to be no way Chitra could reach him.

By the end of 1992, Kohli stopped working with HMV, donning the mantle of a consultant instead. But he managed to persuade Jagjit to work on an album titled *Rare Gems*, where he would compile the songs Jagjit and Chitra had sung in EPs and trace the evolution of the singers through the years. 'Jagjit demurred at first, saying that his voice was different then, his style yet to evolve, but once we cleaned up the old numbers and the CD was released, it proved to be quite a treasure for his fans.' The album included gems like '*Dhuan uttha*' and '*Unki hasrat hai*'.

Jagjit would find support in Monica, who helped him negotiate the agony that still consumed him from within.

Monica, in *Beyond Time*,* mentions that a friend came across to her, three days after her brother's death, with a message from him. She accompanied him to meet the lady who had received the message. They held a séance. 'At first, I thought my communication with my brother was all in my mind, not really with him, but I was given such details by him as to what actually happened in the crash, who had come in, who had stolen stuff, all details which I have been able to verify.'

According to Chitra, 'Mini and I got into spiritual contact. We started regularly visiting Nanny Umrigar, who was the mother of the jockey Karl Umrigar, who had also died when he was about nineteen. She was doing automatic writing, connecting with her son.' Jagjit was intrigued, and soon joined them. Chitra continued to communicate with Baboo through Nanny. Even after she returned home, she would get messages asking her to do things. Chitra remembers how they had amazing and inexplicable experiences connected with her son. Soon she sought out others, hungry now for continued contact.

Vivek's passing was a turning point in the lives of his parents. They turned spiritual, a fact that also reflected in Jagjit's future recordings.

'Mrs Rishi was another person we took to visiting,' Chitra remembers. 'She had started the Theosophical Society in Bombay, which had attracted members like Arthur Conan Doyle and Madame Blavatsky. She lived in a tiny, ramshackle place in Opera House.

'We went to her, seeking closer contact with Baboo. The steps to her home were really rickety, they would shift under our weight. But we were so fixed on our mission, it did not matter one bit. And when we finally came face to face with her, we could not believe this was the person we had come to see. She was so tiny—an eighty-two-year-old, very bent and faded.'

Mrs Rishi used the planchet to communicate with the spirits of the dead. 'She would do table tapping. It was amazing. What she spelt out

Shadowed by grief

was fantastic. But Papa was not convinced. He would keep looking under the table, and even I would sometimes wonder. But slowly our conviction grew, and we were drawn into it. Our need to believe was so great.

'There were plenty of indications that Baboo was trying to stay in touch, to tell us something. It was as if he wanted us to know he was with us always. Once when a college friend of his came to see us, the fragrance of his aftershave suddenly filled the room. She(Mrs Rishi) smelt it too, and asked me if I could smell it. I said, "Yes, he is with us."

'If it were not for these communications, I would never have recovered from the depression I had sunk into. I still missed touching him, or feeding him. But I began to hope to be able to speak directly with him some day. I developed faith because I had no other option; it was a lifeline.'

Then one day, a new line of communication seemed to open up.

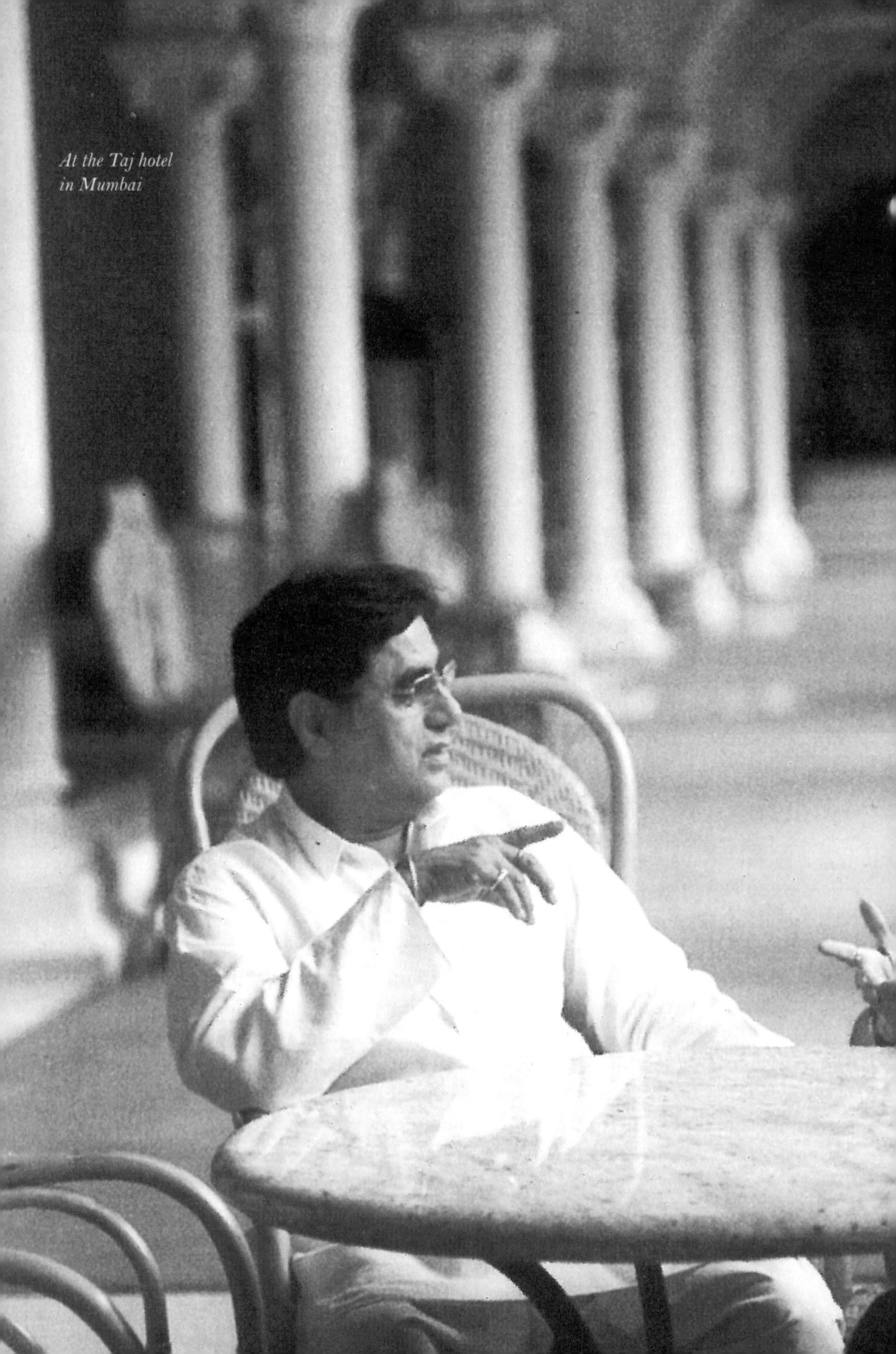

At the Taj hotel in Mumbai

'IF IT WERE NOT FOR THESE COMMUNICATIONS, I WOULD NEVER HAVE RECOVERED FROM THE DEPRESSION I HAD SUNK INTO. I STILL MISSED TOUCHING HIM, OR FEEDING HIM. BUT I BEGAN TO HOPE TO BE ABLE TO SPEAK DIRECTLY WITH HIM SOME DAY. I DEVELOPED FAITH BECAUSE I HAD NO OTHER OPTION; IT WAS A LIFELINE.'

LIKE MOTHER LIKE DAUGHTER. MONICA WITH CHITRA SINGH.

'Mini got home a brochure. It was about Arthur Findlay College of Spiritualism and Psychic Sciences in Stanstead, in Essex, near Cambridge, England. As Monica was psychic to a degree, and dabbled in tarot cards which she read rather accurately, she was keen to attend a course over there. She enrolled and left, but three days into the course, she called up, excitedly saying, "You have got to come. You and Papa. You must arrive within this date," she added, giving a particular date, and asked us to book an appointment with Gordon Higginson, the principal. He was considered the world over as the one medium who could perform a physical manifestation.'

Jagjit and Chitra booked their tickets and, on reaching, enrolled into the seven-day, twenty-four-hour residential learning system, and started attending classes.

However, they were to be disappointed. Higginson had recently had a heart attack and had been forbidden to try physical manifestations. In a physical manifestation, ectoplasm emanates from the medium and manifests as the dead person. It is an exhausting and demanding process and Higginson ran the risk of dying if he tried.

Higginson gave them time for a long sitting, though. He agreed to act as the medium, though forbidden from being the conduit for physical manifestations. Chitra recollects that their session with him left her feeling that she was indeed in contact with Baboo.

Besides the wonderful sitting with Higginson, they also interacted with many other mediums. After completing the course, the Singhs returned.

Once back, they used to fix a time of the day to hold their communications with Baboo. This became a daily routine until Jagjit, finally getting impatient to shed the mood he had lived in and now ready to move on, told Chitra to do the sessions alone, and made plans to travel.

Once again the Singhs' paths that had met briefly had diverged, leading them in different directions.

Kisi ranjish ko hawa do ke main zinda hoon abhi
Mujh ko ehsas dila do ke main zinda hoon abhi

Mere rukne se meri saansein bhi ruk jaayengi
Faasle aur badha do ke main zinda hoon abhi

Zehar peeney ki to aadat thi zamaane vaalon
Ab koi aur dawa do ke main zinda hoon abhi

Chalti raahon mein yunhi aankh lagi hai Faakir
Bheed logon ki hata do ke main zinda hoon abhi

JAGJIT LEANT TOWARDS THE SPIRITUAL TO INCLUDE ALL PHILOSOPHI
AT A FUNCTION DEDICATED TO THE MOTHER AND SRI AUROBINDO.

A person is remembered by what he does. If he makes a mark that is indelible in any field, people remember him long after he is gone. Sometimes the memory endures, even though tastes may change and new notions of what is great and what is not may emerge.

Others are remembered for the goodness of their heart. The things they shared, the aura they cast on the lives of others and the helping hand they held out to those in need, immortalize them.

Perhaps, one of the reasons that Jagjit Singh's fan following is so unique is the fact that in his lifetime, he combined both qualities.

In his art, he was unrelenting, pursuing excellence till the last day of his life, never accepting anything less than perfect from himself. Though he extended himself beyond singing to composing, arranging and ensuring all other aspects of transforming a composition into a marketable commodity, he never sacrificed the purity of his art for the sake of the marketplace.

The second reason was his ability to reach out and touch the lives of all those he sensed needed him. Kuldeep Desai, who was Jagjit's manager for over two decades, tells of the time Jagjit had recorded the album *Hey Ram*.

'It was a bestseller, and Jagjit had written most of it himself. Faakir contributed only a small portion. He also composed and arranged the music for the album, as he always did. If you look at the inlay card, however, you will notice that the lyrics are attributed to Sudarshan Faakir. Jagjit did not want credit for the lyrics, one, because he was not a known lyricist, and two, as he put it, he did not want to be a Manoj Kumar, "doing everything from start to finish and putting my name down the entire list". Sudarshan's name, he felt, would also add commercial viability.

'About five years ago, he came to know that Faakir was trying to build a house and needed money for it. Jagjit rang up HMV and asked them to pay the royalties for *Hey Ram* to Faakir. Of course, after his call, HMV paid up. The amount was close to ten lakhs. I asked him, "Why give that to Faakir when you wrote the lyrics?" He said, "But his name went on it. Maybe the album did well on the strength of his name." He never even asked Faakir for the money back. It was amazing how softly he deflected the issue.'

Both aspects of Jagjit's persona changed with his son's death. The music changed. He drifted into new realms, and his songs became

Kirtans, shabads, songs in praise of gods, Jagjit sang them all

more introspective, more spiritual. Jagjit's early singing of the shabads had honed the spiritual bent of his mind to a level where he wasn't even aware that much of his singing was like a communication with the Divine. Now in his new phase of a man deceived by life, his songs took on serious spiritual overtones, and he found himself reaching out to lyrics that spoke of human life in a contemplative context.

In the early 1990s, Chitra and Jagjit had sung bhajans for *Samarpan*, perhaps the first ever bhajan album. Even at that time, the bhajans had carried with them the incense of true devotion and faith in their words. Among the contents was the Sri Krishna Mahamantra, and listening to Jagjit Singh chant it, according to Swami Suradas of ISKCON, was 'as if the special light of the Lord was coming through him'.

Through the 2000s, Jagjit sang for discs with titles like *Kirtan*, *Aum*, *Radhe Krishna Radhe Shyam* and *Shiva*.

Then, something changed.

Like a man swept by winds that buffeted him as they pleased, he also went from one recording company

Covers of Jagjit's spiritual releases

to another, no longer choosy or particular about what he created. 'If a record company approached him, he would sift through his pre-recorded music and randomly pick out eight songs to present to them. It meant much money, but I don't know if that mattered to him either,' Sanjeev Kohli says of this phase.

In the decade of the new millennium, Jagjit Singh released records through Tips, Venus and a host of other music houses. The lyrics became less meaningful, they beat about the tried and tested themes of wine, romantic longing and love. Jagjit just did not seem to care any more, a tiredness had set in. There was a repetitiveness that seemed to have entered his compositions, as if he had lost his way and was taking repeated U-turns. Despite the public's continued adulation, his new releases did only middling business. Many would soon be forgotten. However, by the time he stopped making albums, he had notched up eighty to his credit. By any count a formidable number, and a long record of creativity.

Prominent political leaders can be counted among Jagjit Singh's

AMONG HIS FANS: THE THEN PRIME MINISTER MANMOHAN SINGH AND HIS WIFE GURSHARAN KAUR WERE AVID LISTENERS. HERE AT THE RELEASE OF THE *SAI DHUN* SPECIAL IN AID OF TSUNAMI VICTIMS

WITH THE THEN PRESIDENT DR A.P.J. ABDUL KALAM

fans. Manmohan Singh invited the Singhs home and confessed that the family listened to no other music but theirs. A.B. Vajpayee, himself a poet, was another aficionado of Jagjit and Chitra Singh. Jagjit repaid the compliment by recording *Samvedna*, with Vajpayee's poetry set to his music.

'*Door kahin koi rota hai*', which Vajpayee wrote in a hospital when he heard relatives of the dead crying on receiving the body, was a poem that touched Jagjit to the quick. Perhaps the kinship he felt with the invisible subjects of the poem was responsible for the fact that he composed the tune for it in twenty minutes. Deepak Pandit, his assistant arranger and a musician, was asked to arrange the music for the melody. The heart-rending flute composition he introduced to support Jagjit's voice would always bring tears to the singer's eyes.

But through the tribulation of continuing a life that brought him little joy, Jagjit never lost his humanity. Sorrow did not embitter him; instead it seemed to spur him to acts of kindness that helped a multitude of people, some of whom he hardly knew. That was the second change.

'Papa learnt it from his father, he would not stint on giving,' as Chitra says, adding that at any given time, there were at least ten families being supported by him.

Kuldeep Desai has an interesting story to share. He had met Jagjit as a bookie; he used to take his bets at the races. 'I was his fan and having learnt classical music myself, music was a passion, and he was my idol.' Wanting to know Jagjit better, Desai offered him more money at the races, and Jagjit took to seeking him out. Their acquaintance grew.

'For some reason, he trusted me. When he was too busy to run his own errands, he would call me to pick up or drop money from his winnings at his home or the Western Outdoor studio.' Something drew Desai to the singer, and he started attending his concerts. 'I would wait

Jagjit leant his voice to Vajpayee's poetry

in the green room and touch his feet. Soon he knew I was a regular. Most of the time he would be too busy to interact with his promoters, and I would be given the task of collecting the money and disbursing it among his accompanists.'

Responding to an unwritten cue, Desai took on the job of Jagjit's manager. 'Nothing was spoken in so many words, nothing was exchanged in writing. *Bas*, I gave up the races and took him on full-time.'

It is from Desai and many of Jagjit's accompanists that the stories about his generosity emerge. Desai tells of one man who approached Jagjit asking him to perform at a concert on his behalf in his hometown. His daughter was getting married; he needed to raise two lakhs for the wedding, and he thought that Jagjit would of course draw packed houses, and he could easily cull a profit of two lakhs from the show proceeds.

'Jagjit heard him out, then looking absent-minded told him, "Yes, but it is risky." Then he asked the man to talk to me. I gave him the technical requirements, and told him to come back after a week, once he had worked things out.

'The day he was to come, Jagjit asked for a box of sweets and placed the two lakhs needed for the wedding in it. When the man arrived, he told him, "It is very risky, what you want to do. Let me think it over." Seeing the man look dejected, Jagjit consoled him saying all would be well and placed the box in his hands saying, "But meanwhile, here are some sweets from me. We'll talk later." The man left, disappointed for the moment. But he must have realized soon that Jagjit had saved him a lot of trouble. It was amazing how he helped someone without a second thought, and yet saved the man from the embarrassment of knowing he had been given money.'

Abhinav Upadhyay, who left his career to be Jagjit Singh's percussionist for many years, remembers how he was hired. 'I had gone to meet him for a trial, but when I reached his house, he was out. Only Chitra was there. I remember I had injured my hands recently in an accident, and she was most concerned.

'When he came, he motioned me to sit and asked if I would play. I played; it was not good, my hands hurt, I was very nervous, but he said "*achcha hai*" and invited me to the studio the next day for a recording. He was recording for the serial *Kahkashan*. Actually, he knew I needed a break, that I was struggling, so he thought let us give him two days' work at least to tide over his troubles for some time. He had an instinctive understanding of such things. The two days stretched to two months.

'He would not let me worry about making mistakes, saying, "who does not make them?" In some ways, he was my guide and management guru.'

Through his career from the 1970s till his last days, Jagjit Singh held his accompanists dear. His needs followed theirs. When on tour, he would ensure their comfort and no one was ever allowed to treat him in a special manner at the cost of his orchestra players.

Upadhyay is not alone in his loyalty to the singer; most of his accompanists remained with him throughout their careers. There are many stories that offer proof of his genuine concern for his musicians during the many tours. Sometimes the schedules would be tiring, with concerts by night and travel by day. But at every stop, the singer would ensure that all the instruments had arrived intact, and would make his own car wait until the instruments and baggage of all his musicians were safely loaded into the vehicles that had come for them. He would take particular care to know what their accommodation and food would be like, and ensure they had vehicles should they wish to go out in their spare time. Sometimes, he would insist on staying in the same hotel as them.

Considering most musicians are often left to fend for themselves, and organizers usually give them secondary status to the lead artiste, Jagjit's attitude and attention to his musicians' comfort often surprised his hosts. But it was something he just refused to compromise on.

Never forgetting his own family, Jagjit continued to support the remaining siblings as and when he felt they required his help. Chitra avers that he gave unstintingly to his family, not questioning whether they needed his help or not. Kartar Singh, the youngest of his brothers, owes the success of his much-acclaimed Chinese restaurant to Jagjit. 'It was he who persuaded me to jump into hoteliering. We had no experience, my partner and I, but he said, "So what? Hire someone who can run it for you." He always saw the positive side of everything. When we moved to Greater Kailash, to start the Hao Shi Nian Nian restaurant, he looked into every aspect of its decor. And he loved coming here for his meals. I cannot but miss him when I eat here myself.'

Equally encompassing was his ability to include everyone he met in

ACCEPTING RECOGNITION FROM SHARAD YADAV,
THEN MINISTER FOR CIVIL AVIATION

AWARDS CAME IN PLENTY

his aura of friendliness. According to Jagpreet Lamba, close associate and impresario, whenever he performed at Siri Fort, where he held most of his Delhi concerts, the entire staff of the auditorium would gather to meet him. 'Even the *safaiwallas* or cleaners, right from the person who ran the auditorium to the gate-keepers, everyone flocked to the gate from where he was to enter, or came backstage for that one chance to spend a little time with him. And he met them all, greeting them with great warmth and patience. He made time for them, whether before or after the concert or during the interval. He felt for them at a human level. That's why they loved him and wanted to stay in touch with him. He was a people's person.'

The Siri Fort Auditorium was possibly Jagjit's favourite. 'The number of his concerts at Siri Fort must equal that of all others who have sung there, put together,' Kartar Singh says. 'Such was his popularity in Delhi that there were lathi charges on occasion to disperse the crowd that blocked the entry, making it difficult for bona fide ticket holders to enter.'

Kartar narrates a story about how once the milling crowds made it impossible for Jagjit's car to reach the gates of the auditorium. 'I was with him in the car. He remained quite calm and phoned the organizers. Soon, they came out and ensured a way was opened up for the car to move. There were three or four people standing at the entrance, who could not enter despite having tickets. Bhai saab heard them out and said, "just wait", and went in. He took the stage and asked the organizers, "Have you sold out? You have made your profit?" The organizers nodded. "Then open the gates and let everyone in," he said. Soon every available space was filled: aisles, balcony, doorways. The VIPs who came late could not enter, let alone take their seats. It was a housefull show in the true sense of the word.' In fact, every show Jagjit did in Delhi after 1982 went housefull.

Among his fans in Delhi are a group of about seven, who despite knowing Kartar as well as the singer, never bought tickets. Regardless of this fact, they attended every show of his. In fact, when the Jagjit Singh Fan Group in Rohtak invited the singer on his birthday, the seven fans also turned up to attend that function. 'They had sworn never to miss a Jagjit Singh show, and they kept it up,' says Kartar. Such was the loyalty the singer commanded. Jagjit's connect with the audiences assumed legendary status.

With his audience, Jagjit Singh would remain calm and friendly. Despite the demands the travel and singing might have made on him, he never stinted on his time with them, patiently signing autographs, believing that an artiste owed it to his fans to connect with them.

When Chitra stopped travelling with him, it made him all the more attractive as a singer and performer. He came into his own, reaching out to his listeners, their love and energy fuelling his need to find a meaning to his continued being. It was as if, in their midst, singing their favourite songs and listening to their applause, he forgot the emptiness that had settled in his heart.

Chitra took a poor view of his playing to the audience. 'All sorts of women would call him. Socialites, women with time on their hands and looking for romance or excitement. They would phone and compliment him, and he would play along on the phone. Of course, I did not like it. When I would tell him that, he would laugh and say, "They are just fans, I don't live with them, do I? There is no harm in making them happy."

'I learnt that there was no point arguing about this; it was his nature. He openly lapped up praise. The problem was that he could not spot the real admirers from the flatterers, who used this weakness of his to exploit him, both emotionally and monetarily. He would respond to them all with his brand of humour and candour.'

She remembers one time when he was openly flirting with a lady caller. 'When he put the receiver down, I said, "Who was that?" He said, "She was someone at the show last evening, and she was singing my praises." I responded, "But you were

Signing autographs for fans

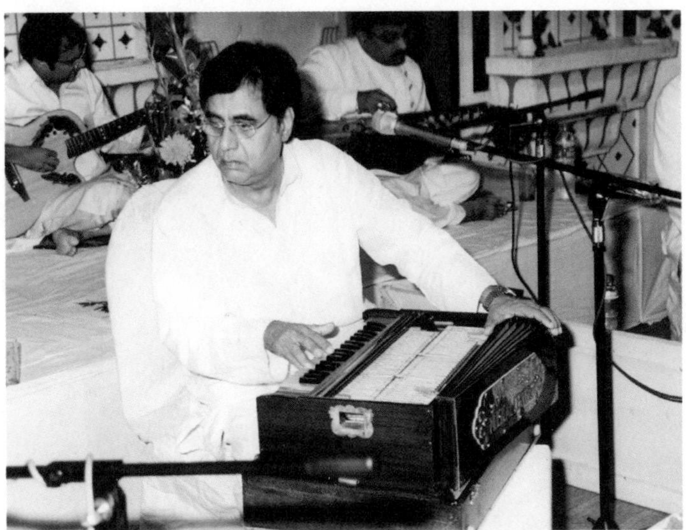

In concert

also flirting with her, why?" and he said, "She was very good looking and she loves my music, so why not. What is the harm in talking?"

'Often he would be invited to dinners, perhaps asked to sing too. I did not like him doing that, accepting just anyone's invitation and going along. But he had stopped caring about what I thought.' At other times, Chitra would rebuke him for changing his mind. 'He would have said yes to someone for a dinner, and then on that day or at the last moment, he would say, "forget it" and stay home. It bothered me a lot.

'And yet he never liked it when I was paid attention. I remember, even before we married, when I was invited to a musician's house in the evening, he wanted to know why I had been invited alone, and said, "Either cancel the appointment, or I will escort you."'

WITH PANKAJ KODESIA

Jagjit's ability to pamper his fans was all encompassing. Jasbir Singh, his friend of many years, has a strange, believe-it-or-not story to share:

'I started playing Jagjit Singh's albums at my restaurant Chenab, when all other types of music failed to impress my clients. I have always been his fan, and wanted desperately for him to visit my restaurant. This seemed like a dream. Then, one day, a man approached me to sponsor a concert by Jagjit in Vashi, Mumbai. I agreed and went, hoping to get a chance to meet him.

'During the interval, with great nervousness, I approached the singer. I expected, of course, to be dealt with in a high-handed manner, and was very happily surprised when he invited me to sit and asked me what I did. I told him I ran a restaurant and invited him to have dinner with me. The organizer who was also present made frantic signals, but Jagjit-ji understood him, and said, "You have not paid me to eat here, I will go to his restaurant."'

That was the start of a twelve-year-long friendship. Jagjit began visiting Chenab regularly. When he went the first time, in 2001, he said, 'The food is good, the ambience is fine, then why is this place not flying?' Then he asked, 'Do you know any TV guys?' Jasbir said that the CEO of a TV channel often ate there. 'Call him,' Jagjit said, 'I want to do a live programme from here.'

Jasbir admits he was terrified that the singer would demand lakhs for the programme. But he made the call anyway, and the next evening was fixed for the event.

To Jasbir's amazement, it all happened like a dream. R.J. Karan recorded Jagjit as he sang at Chenab. And then the singer went on to say over the mike, live to his listeners, 'I am here at Chenab, the food is good, it is cheap,' and then started singing again. The show went on for three hours.

'When it was over, I was overwhelmed. I went up to him, and stammered a thank you and was going to ask him what he was to be paid. But he pre-empted me and said, "This is a gift." But naturally, as was expected, Chenab took off as a popular eating place, and has a huge clientele still.'

Two or three years later, Jagjit repeated the show. 'He just said, "Let's do it again," and did it. I represent some co-op housing societies, he would come and perform for them, too, for free.'

Jasbir became one of Jagjit Singh's closest friends. The friendship was to lead to one of the musician's most significant assignments.

'In 2008, I started representing the Nanded Gurdwara as an advisor. The 300th anniversary of the Gurta Gaddi of Sri Guru Granth Sahib-ji was being planned and they were thinking of an album of the Gurbani with twenty singers singing in it. Thirty-two shabads would be sung by the stalwarts of music. Jagjit Singh got instantly interested. For one-and-a-half years, he worked on the music. Many a time, he would refuse a show because he was engrossed in composing for it. He gave it top preference. When the recording started, he was there full-time, arranging every piece till he was completely satisfied. Chitra would come to the studio and say, "Arre, you will make a jogi out of him." Dr Gunam Singh of Patiala also helped a lot.

'When the album was ready, we got Sonia Gandhi to release it. We also used the fact that a postage stamp was being released on the anniversary to have one released in Jagjit's honour. But our greatest moment came when he went to visit the then Prime Minister, Manmohan Singh, and his wife said, "Please send me a new album, the old one has been played so many times that it has practically rubbed off."

'Jagjit-ji understood I could organize things well, and joined the

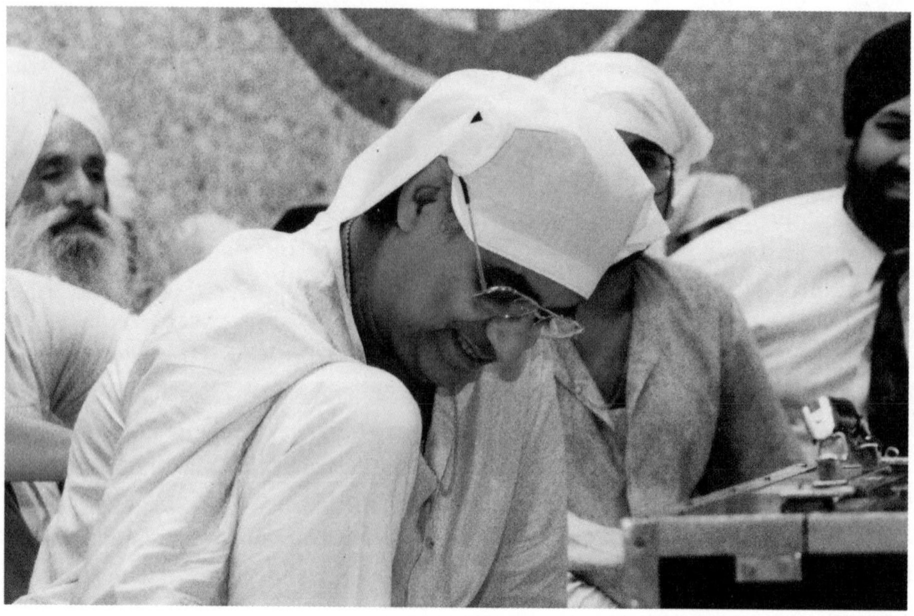

At the Nanded Gurdwara in 2008

Jagjit was very comfortable around children. Here in the audience for a change at a school function.

effort. We planned to build a musical fountain, and have laser shows on the ten gurus. To understand how these could be done, we went to Sentosa in Singapore, where the Songs of the Sea show had all these elements. I had booked a separate room for him. When we were checking in, he said, "Why a separate room, we can share." That night he asked me if I had tea or coffee in the mornings. I said I preferred tea. Did I have bed tea? I said yes. The next morning he stood by my bed with a cup of tea in hand.

'It did not stop there. As I was bathing, he knocked to ask what I planned to wear. He was ironing his clothes and could do mine too. I came out in a towel to stop him, but he would not stop till my clothes were well pressed and folded.

'He was so down-to-earth. Often when we were coming from the suburbs and we would reach Kalanagar in East Bandra, he knew I had to go to Vashi, in the opposite direction. So he would get down and try and get a rickshaw. I would pull him back, and insist on dropping him home. He would resist. It used to be quite a *tamasha* on the road.'

Sometimes Jagjit Singh's reaching out to fans and friends would rebound on him. Abhinav Upadhyay remembers a time when Jagjit was to perform at a function that he had organized. 'Tridhara was an ambitious programme I had organized. The seats were sold out

At Niagara Falls

'HE WAS SO DOWN-TO-EARTH. OFTEN WHEN WE WERE COMING FROM THE SUBURBS AND WE WOULD REACH KALANAGAR IN EAST BANDRA, HE KNEW I HAD TO GO TO VASHI, IN THE OPPOSITE DIRECTION. SO HE WOULD GET DOWN AND TRY AND GET A RICKSHAW. I WOULD PULL HIM BACK, AND INSIST ON DROPPING HIM HOME. HE WOULD RESIST. IT USED TO BE QUITE A *TAMASHA* ON THE ROAD.'

MUSIC AT HIS FINGERTIPS

Postage stamps issued in Jagjit Singh's honour

well in advance. The show was to start at 6.30 p.m. I confirmed with Jagjit-ji that all was well at around 4.30 p.m. As the time for the show drew near, I called him, and, to my dismay, his phone was switched off. I was at the venue, unable to go across and check what the matter was. The show started on time, Hari-ji was close to finishing his piece by 7.30 p.m. and there was still no sign of Jagjit-ji. At 7.45 p.m. he called me, saying he was walking up. I said, "This is all for you, where are you?" He walked in then from backstage, a shawl covering his head. All went well, and the audience was thrilled. But I wonder what around fifty of his fans and friends would have thought of him. As he explained, he had switched off his phone to avoid their calls. When they had called earlier asking for seats, he had generously told them, "Meet me outside the theatre, I will take you in," not realizing till that afternoon, that the hall was full, and every seat had been sold out.'

IN HAPPIER TIMES

Perhaps the most significant service done to the ghazal by Jagjit Singh were the recordings tracing the history of the genre, on which he collaborated with Gulzar.

Already, his contribution to the art form had been nationally recognized, with the conferring of the Padma Bhushan Award on him in 2003. Jagjit Singh shared the honour with Naseeruddin Shah and Amir Khan, and received the award from A.P.J. Abdul Kalam. The collection that HMV planned would highlight his place in the history of the ghazal.

'Jagjit could play favourites with artistes and songs, so I got in Gulzar as a balancing factor,' Sanjeev Kohli remembers, as he rewinds to the recording of the *Ghazal Ka Safar* series. The cassettes had an introduction of each artiste by Jagjit, which I scripted. As EMI Pakistan was an affiliate of HMV India, the collection also included Pakistani singers like Noor Jehan. The series did phenomenally well, thanks mostly to Jagjit and Gulzar and the USP they brought to the series. It was also transferred on to a CD collection, but as the contract with EMI Pakistan did not cover CDs, the singers from there had to be left out. Despite this, the two introducers made for such good listening that the CDs were also a hit.'

The poet-singer combination worked wonderfully on stage too. 'When I first suggested to Gulzar that he do a stage show with Jagjit-ji, he demurred. "I am a serious kind of man," he said, "why will the audience listen to me? Jagjit will come on stage and sing a *tappa*, and the audience will be floored." Surprisingly, Jagjit was also hesitant, saying that Gulzar's aura was so powerful, the audience would be floored and not pay him any attention. However, the shows did happen, and became something that audiences flocked to.'

Gulzar recounts how at one of their collaborative programmes together at Siri Fort, Jagjit kept repeating two lines of a ghazal at the end, his eyes shining with mischief. 'I realized it was my cue to enter. When I entered the stage, he said, much to the delight of the audience, "Did you understand my *ishara*?" Our shows were full of such give and take, the audiences of course loved them.'

Jagjit continued to perform, regardless of health problems. He never grew breathless as singers who age or suffer from heart problems do. His voice remained the same. On his seventieth birthday, in 2011, he decided to hold seventy concerts through the year. This meant an average of more than five in a month. It was a tough assignment that he gave himself, but it was possibly his way of negating the barbs life was still aiming at him.

Jagjit had not quite come to terms with the death of Monica, whom he had regarded as his own daughter through their years together.

Monica, who remained close to Jagjit and Chitra, was a popular model thanks to her petite but near-perfect figure and astounding good looks. Ex-model Arti Surendranath, who was also modelling around the same time, remembers how she would look with awe upon Monica, who, as the older and more experienced of the two, carried herself with an unmistakably sophisticated air.

Monica, loved and lost

'More than her looks, it was her chutzpah that struck you,' Arti recalls. 'She had a great sense of humour, was always saying things that made us crack up. She was a comic, even her speech had a laugh bubbling in it. It was so sad that by the time her boys grew old enough, she had become quite a changed person. Even when her emotional life was a mess, she would laugh about it; she was one of those rare people who know how to laugh at themselves.'

Arti also recounts how when *India Today* was doing a cover story on models, most of whom were getting upset over the obnoxious personal questions being put to them, Monica managed to turn them into a laughing matter. 'I had carried a dress I had made. I used to stitch in those days. She picked it up and insisted on wearing it. When I remonstrated, she said, "What rubbish, we cannot let it go to waste, can we?" And believe it or not, it was her in that dress, who out of all of us, including some senior models, made it to the cover of that issue.

'It was common knowledge among her friends that she was going through an emotional crisis, but no one expected her to go so far; the news of her suicide was a huge shock.'

Monica's husband Jehangir Chowdhury with their sons in Mauritius

Monica had two sons through her marriage with Jehangir Chowdhury, a cinematograper. The two had divorced due to irreconciliable differences only to marry again, and divorce once more. Monica had then married a British national, Mark Atkins. According to a news report posted in *India Forums*, 'The marriage, however, had also turned sour and Monica was forced to lodge a dowry torture case against Atkins in September 2007, alleging assault and harassment. The litigation had been running since then and it had robbed Monica of her peace of mind.'

Monica's resultant suicide in 2009 at the age of forty-nine, by hanging herself from a fan with her dupatta, scarred Jagjit and Chitra further. Jagjit immersed himself in his music, planning whirlwind tours to keep himself occupied. Only Monica's boys, Armaan and Umer, could make him relax the stance he had put up against life. He moved to the Bandra residence to join the children and Chitra, who had already moved there, while Monica was alive, to help her tackle depression. 'However paradoxical it may sound, it's true that all the spiritual awareness and wisdom

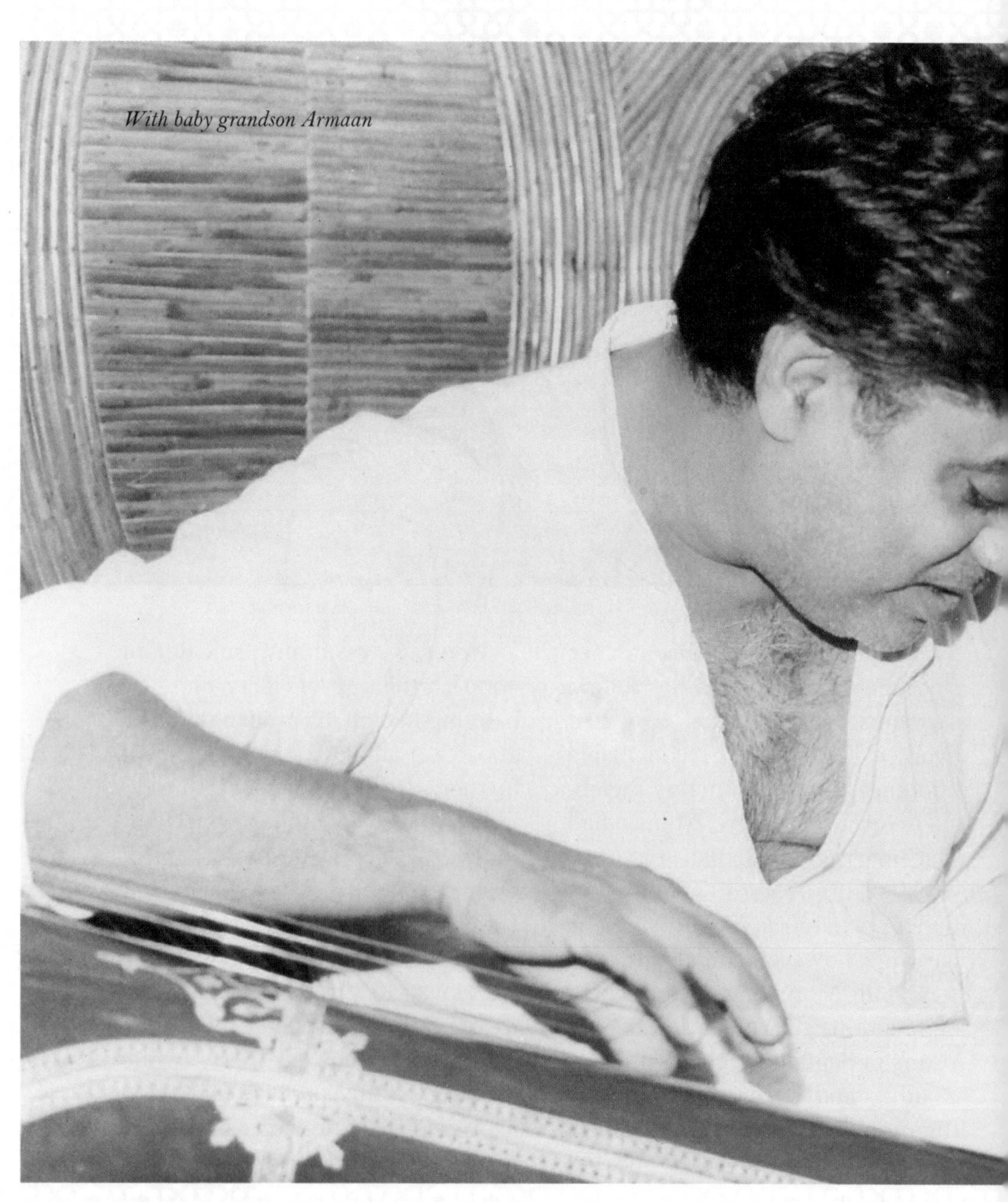

With baby grandson Armaan

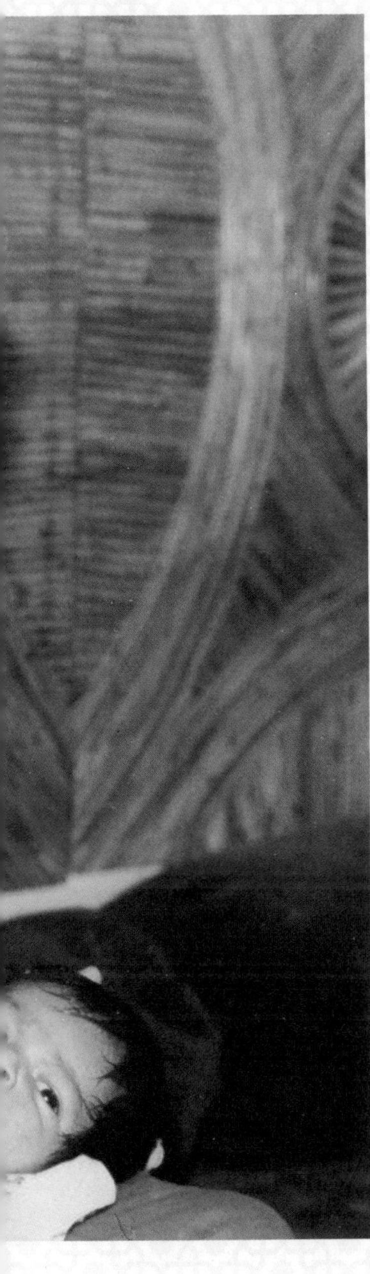

JAGJIT IMMERSED HIMSELF IN HIS MUSIC, PLANNING WHIRLWIND TOURS TO KEEP HIMSELF OCCUPIED. ONLY MONICA'S BOYS, ARMAAN AND UMER, COULD MAKE HIM RELAX THE STANCE HE HAD PUT UP AGAINST LIFE.

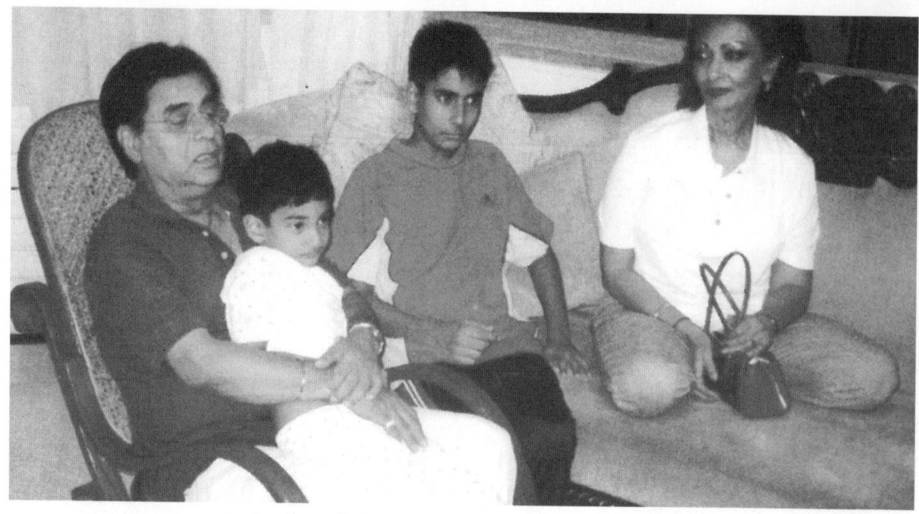

Jagjit and Chitra with their beloved grandsons

that I have today was instilled in me by Monica. Today, not only her children but I, too, feel lost without her loving guidance,' says Chitra.

All through the first half of 2011, Jagjit Singh toured the country tirelessly, accompanied by his faithful band of musicians. He was performing till almost the last day before he fell mortally ill.

His charity performances too continued. The multitalented actor Dolly Thakore remembers the fact that, despite his own tragedies, Jagjit Singh reached out to help others. 'He came without fuss every time we asked him to sing for a fundraiser for Alert India. He never asked for things like transport, or even discussed a fee. He would come and sing and whether it was the Shanmukhananda or Bhaidas auditoriums we had booked for the show, we would have a packed house. Which would really be a great bonanza for us. The only concert he missed was the last one, because it was scheduled just four days before his death, by which time he was in hospital, battling for his life. Alert India lost a champion when he went; his espousal of the cause was so genuine. He even spent time with the leprosy afflicted, much to their delight.'

'He still had musical dreams he wished to turn into reality,' Sood recalls. While they were in London, Jagjit had planned an ambitious project wherein he would sing to a packed audience with the London Philharmonic Orchestra playing behind him in surround sound. 'It would cost almost a crore to make it happen, but he was very keen on it. But once he came back, he was sucked into performances, recordings and the nitty-gritty of life, and so the project hung fire. He needed to be pushed to do it, and that somehow did not happen.'

Other dreams took the place of those abandoned unrealized. Kuldeep Desai recalls that, 'Through 16, 17, 18 September, he pushed himself beyond his own limits. He performed at Nehru Centre in Mumbai on the 16th, then at Siri Fort the next day, and at Karnal on the 18th. On the 19th, he went by road to Dehradun for a show on the 20th. I accompanied him there and then returned to Mumbai. On the 21st, he was to come back to Delhi for an award function.

'He called me on the 22nd, saying "I'm in Mumbai, I did not go to Delhi. I am not feeling well." He added that he would rest and call me in the evening.'

Jasbir Singh remembers calling him on 21 September. 'He had called my less-used phone repeatedly, and when I noticed the call, I called him back asking if I should come to Worli and meet him. He told me not to come to Worli but to Bandra. He was taking Chitra to the Lilavati Hospital. It was nothing serious, and he would meet me on his return.

'We met at 8 p.m. and sat upstairs, drinking Kashmiri kahwa. Chitra was in and out of the room, so he did not say much, though I could guess he was holding back some excitement. I wondered what it was.

'"Would you like to start an open-air restaurant?" he asked me half-jokingly. "I am looking at some places where we can enjoy open spaces and fresh air. *Aage ki zindagi khuli hawa mein jeeyunga*," he said, throwing his arms out expansively.

'He was to perform with Ghulam Ali the next day. Around the time of the concert, I got a call from RJ Gaurav Sharma of Fever 104 FM. "Jagjit Singh has cancelled the concert," he said, "he is not well." I said it was Chitra who was not well, and he replied that Jagjit had been rushed to hospital—he had had a stroke.

'Exactly ninety minutes after he told me he wanted to breathe in fresh air and live the rest of his life in open spaces, Jagjit Singh was encased in the glass-walled confines of an ICU. Lilavati Hospital was on red alert. Even the first floor was cordoned off to prevent fans and friends from crowding in. Only Chitra was permitted outside the ICU. But multiple surgeries and all other efforts to revive the singer proved in vain. He breathed his last on 10 October 2011.'

He was never to emerge into the living world again.